Banana George!
*Don't Wait for Life to Happen
Make it Happen*

The Blair Family

JoAnne Blair,
Donna Blair, Georgia Blair,
Carrie Blair, Robin Blair

with
Karen Putz

Foreword by Phil Keoghan

Banana George!: Don't Wait for Life to Happen Make it Happen

Copyright © 2018 by Georgia Blair

All rights reserved. No part of this book may be used or reproduced by any means, graphic, electronic, or mechanical, including photocopying, recording, taping, or by any information storage retrieval system without the written permission of the publisher except in the case of brief quotations embodied in critical articles and reviews.

Email inquiries should be addressed to:
barefoot@bananageorgeblair.com

Facebook: https://www.facebook.com/BananaGeorgeBlair/

Website: www.BananaGeorgeBlair.com

ISBN: 978-0-692-99660-7

Cover Photo Credit: Cy Cyr

Editor: Tyler Tichelaar, Superior Book Productions

Layout: Larry Alexander, Superior Book Productions

All attempts have been made to source properly each quote.

What People Are Saying About Banana George

Banana George was the best ambassador that water skiing ever had. His high visibility (yellow) could be found on TV commercials, billboards, advertisements, magazine and newspaper stories around the world.

Scott N. Atkinson, Editor, *The Water Skier* magazine

I have skied with George, and hung out with him for many years, and he has always been an inspiration for me. George is a great example of someone who has lived his life to the fullest, and has been a great influence on many people around the world.

Mike Seipel, 2x World Barefoot Champion

Since I was eleven years old, Banana George has been an icon in the sport of barefoot waterskiing. Not only did he sign thousands and thousands of autographs, but he also contributed monetarily to the sport. He was a remarkable man and always positive in everything he did, both on the water and off. This book is a wonderful example of how we can continue to learn and grow, no matter our age.

Keith St. Onge, 18x US National Overall Champion, 15x World Champion Gold Medalist

As far back as I can remember since I started to barefoot, Banana George was in the spotlight. Every time I met him, he was happy, energetic, and extremely enthusiastic about the sport. He was and always will be someone I looked up to. He showed everyone that age is simply a number and that the only limits we have are what we put upon ourselves.

David Small, 6x World Barefoot Champion

For me, Banana George Blair was not only the man in yellow—he was *the golden man*, with soul and inspiration for our wonderful sport.

Franz Kirsch, 1st Chairman of the barefoot division of International Wasserski Wakeboard Federation (IWWF), Editor of *Wasserski Magazine*

The legend of Mr. Blair. What a career, what a man, and what an enduring life he lived with tremendous passion. If ole Banana was still around, I'd kiss his feet and congratulate him for inspiring millions of people to pursue their passions.

Todd Ristorcelli, former WATERSKI magazine editor-in-chief

Banana George was an icon in water ski barefooting. At age seventy-five, he learned to snowboard. He became Steamboat's Honorary Snowboard Ambassador, and my close friend. He loved to share his enthusiasm. His life was an inspiration to me and his story will be an inspiration to you.

Billy Kidd, Olympic Skiing Medalist and World Champion

George and I worked together at Cypress Gardens for many years but I don't think he ever considered it work. He loved performing—he was a true showman—he loved the crowds and the adulation. Even when the weather was terrible and the audience discouraged, I would send George out first to pull the show together. He never tired of interacting with others to promote the sport that was his lifeblood. George proved that greatness comes from serving others while doing what you love!

Lynn Novakofski, former Cypress Gardens Show Director, Photography/Graphics USA Water Ski

This man is doing phenomenal things past the age of ninety. Without question, his performances are "world class" and I "tell his story" to people all over the world.

Dr. Kenneth Cooper, Cooper Institute and Clinic in Dallas, Texas

When you're a barefoot skier like I am, you live life large and want to be Banana George when you grow up—and never grow old. He was iconic in the sport, but you may not know how the passion he showed on the water extended to *every* area of his life. This book will inspire you to follow his example by squeezing all you can out of each opportunity you get.

Dave Ramsey, best-selling author and nationally syndicated radio show host

George Blair was a lifelong friend, mentor, and inspiration. His zest for life and health were an example that influenced how I live. His enthusiasm for his endeavors was inspirational and contagious. George truly redefined what aging meant for millions.

Ron Scarpa, 4x World Barefoot Champion, 13x US National Overall Champion, 2017 International Waterski & Wakeboard Hall of Fame

Never Too Late

Henry Wadsworth Longfellow (1874)
(excerpted from 24 stanzas)

It is too late! Ah, nothing is too late
Till the tired heart shall cease to palpitate.

Cato learned Greek at eighty; Sophocles
Wrote his grand Oedipus, and Simonides

Bore off the prize of verse from his compeers,
When each had numbered more than fourscore years,

And Theophrastus, at fourscore and ten,
Had but begun his "Characters of Men."

Chaucer, at Woodstock with the nightingales,
At sixty wrote the Canterbury Tales;

Goethe at Weimar, toiling to the last,
Completed Faust when eighty years were past.

What then? Shall we sit idly down and say
The night hath come; it is no longer day?

For age is opportunity no less
Than youth itself, though in another dress,

And as the evening twilight fades away
The sky is filled with stars, invisible by day.

It is never too late to start doing what is right.
Never.

Contents

Foreword i
Preface iii
Introduction: The Showman v
Section I: The Early Years 1
    Chapter 1: Growing Up 3
    Chapter 2: Love in Bloom 7
    Chapter 3: Becoming a Dad 15
    Chapter 4: The Birth of an Entrepreneur 19
    Chapter 5: A Barefoot Water Skier Is Born 27
    Chapter 6: Blair Family Rhythm 39
Section II: Fame and Change 53
    Chapter 7: Changing Course 55
    Chapter 8: Relentless Tenacity 61
    Chapter 9: Becoming Banana George 67
    Chapter 10: Yellow Fever 73
    Chapter 11: Around the World on Water Skis 79
Section III: A New Focus 107
    Chapter 12: Florida to Antarctica to Russia with Love 109
    Chapter 13: Barefooting in Finland and Switzerland 121
    Chapter 14: Becoming a Hall-of-Famer 127
    Chapter 15: Daredevil and Movie Star 135
    Chapter 16: Skiing for the King 141
    Chapter 17: Renaissance Man 145
    Chapter 18: Bulls and Broken Backs 155
    Chapter 19: Media Star 159
    Chapter 20: Ninety Years Young 165
    Chapter 21: Unstoppable 171
    Chapter 22: All Good Things Come to an End 177
Banana George's Lessons on Life 183
Countries Where Banana George Skied and/or Barefoot Water Skied.....184
Businesses Owned by Banana George 185
Banana George's : Affiliations and Memberships 186
Contributors 188
Bibliography 190
About the Authors 192

Foreword

I OFTEN TELL people I want to be just like Banana George when I grow up, living each day as if it were my last, filled with laughter, enthusiasm, and appreciation for all our blessings. I have a signed postcard from George in my office that proudly displays his age as eighty-three and three months, a constant reminder that our age should be seen as a badge of honor, not a curse. This was a message George loved sharing with everyone he met.

They say that to be a master at anything, you need to practice at least 10,000 hours. Perhaps George was the world's greatest master of optimism…honed from decades of living positively. It all stemmed from his genuine fascination and love of people. George certainly caught people's attention with his passion for yellow but, ultimately, it was his magnetic personality and sparkle in his eye that really enthralled everyone he met.

When you were with George, you instinctively found yourself smiling with an overwhelming feeling that you could do anything you put your mind to and you shouldn't waste another minute. George helped me understand that we should all focus on what we have and can do, rather than what we don't have and can't do. He solidified my personal philosophy of living in the *N.O.W., No Opportunity Wasted*.

George epitomized what it meant to live a full and productive life. He lived by example, proving that age is just a number and that attitude is everything. I remember he once said, *"You know me. I like to be individualistic!"*…and he was; there will never be another Banana George. He shared his life secrets starting with thinking young, drinking lots of water, eating bananas and vegetables, exercising, trying new things, taking off your shoes whenever possible, and connecting with people.

I feel honored to have shared some amazing life moments with him, and now you can too! After reading this book, I am certain you'll think of Banana George whenever you hear someone say, "*I'm too old for that!*"

By Phil Keoghan

@PhilKeoghan

Phil, from New Zealand, is a renowned adventurer, producer, writer, actor, cameraman, and the host of the Emmy Award-winning series *The Amazing Race* on CBS—a show that has won the Outstanding Reality-Competition Program many times. He is the author and creator of *No Opportunity Wasted*.

Preface

Our dad, "Banana" George Blair, was a prolific note taker and statistician. He saved his personal letters, essays, school report cards, calendars, diaries (1935-1937), employment records, business correspondence, health reports, and photographs. He accumulated voluminous files of articles written about his accomplishments. His archives showed us that he wanted his story told. This is our heartfelt effort to present an overview of his life. To us, he was an adorable, eccentric dad. In reviewing his life, we were amazed at his prominence and positive impact on people around the world.

People asked him, "What is your secret? How do you defy your age?"

What makes his life story so compelling?

We think it was possibly the trauma he experienced at seven years old when his favorite brother died of diabetes, untreatable in 1922, and his disabling back condition that, when fixed, catapulted him into a fast track to achieve his endless goals. We believe these circumstances inspired him to accomplish enough for two lifetimes. He lived almost a century—from when owning a car was a privilege, well before television was invented, until smart phones were in everyone's hands. His story has the power to reach everyone who looks for a hero.

JoAnne, his devoted wife for forty years, contributed many stories of their action-packed life. Her perennial optimism facilitated the realization of his relentless pursuits.

We asked Karen Putz, a writer and barefoot water skier, for help in telling this story. She interviewed dozens of people and created a format on which we could build. The result is the book in your hands. We hope it inspires you to live life to its fullest. We know that is what Banana George would wish for you.

Introduction
The Showman

On a hot summer day, a long line of people snaked into the stands in Winter Haven, Florida. The temperature registered 97°, but the crowd did not seem to mind. They were standing in line to see one of the longest-running theatrical acts on water: the Cypress Gardens Water Ski Show.

"Ladies and gentlemen, take your seats, please. The show is about to begin."

A little over 2,500 people were jammed elbow-to-elbow in front of the lake. The chatter quieted down when a clown came on stage to entertain the kids with clumsy antics.

"Could I have a volunteer from the audience, please?" the announcer asked. A show of hands went up. The announcer scanned the crowd and selected an elderly man sitting in the front to the left. He was dressed in yellow from head to toe, with yellow sunglasses perched on his nose. The man slowly shuffled his way to the dock, his silver-gray hair gleaming in the sun. The announcer handed a water ski handle to the man and proceeded to explain the nuances of water skiing. The man took off his sunglasses and handed them to the announcer as he struggled to follow the instructions on how to maintain proper water skiing form.

The other end of the ski rope was connected to a long white boat with two enormous motors perched on the stern. All at once, music blared from the loudspeakers and the boat took off at full speed. The crowd gasped when the old man still holding the ski handle was jerked off his feet, running toward the water. The man took a flying leap and landed with a splash on his back in the water. A few seconds later, the man stood up—water skiing on his own two feet. As he passed the crowd, he held the handle with his teeth and stretched both arms out wide.

The applause thundered. The man skied on his bare feet around the lake, then gracefully glided to the shore. He waved to the stunned audience with a big smile on his face.

Next, a group of skiers took to the water, performing various stunts. Another round of skiers came out—this time it was a ballet line of women dressed in beautiful swimsuits and flowing skirts. They swiveled gracefully to music piped out from the stage. Men on large skis jumped off the ramp, crisscrossing each other before landing with a splash and skiing away. As soon as one boat passed by, another boat took off with the next round of skiers. A line of muscular men shouldered beautiful women, forming a pyramid four tiers high.

As soon as the show was over, the crowd swarmed around the elderly man in yellow, clamoring for an autograph, a picture, and a few words of inspiration and praise. "How did you do that at your age?" they wanted to know. Laughing and smiling, he answered their questions one by one and handed out bananas to everyone who approached him.

"Who's that man in yellow?" a little boy asked his mom.

"That's Banana George."

Section I
The Early Years

1915–1973

"Happiness is not what you have,
but how you enjoy what you have."

— "Banana" George Blair

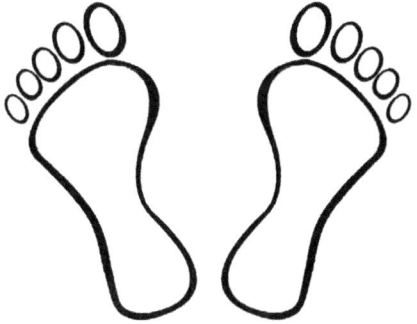

Chapter 1

Growing Up

On January 22, 1915, a colorful entrepreneur was born.

George Blair, later known as "Banana George," completely redefined aging and demonstrated how to live a full life. In his sixties, seventies, eighties, and nineties, he was constantly reinventing himself and seizing every chance to learn new things. He was quite the colorful guy—not only because he dressed from head-to-toe in yellow—but because his enthusiasm and energy painted a wonderful picture of what life can be when you live full out. Imagine a life where you skydive, ride a camel, drive a race car, snow board, snow ski with Billy Kidd, and water ski on your bare feet behind a plane, all at the age of eighty-plus.

There's a saying by the poet Diane Ackerman, "I don't want to get to the end of my life and find that I just lived the length of it. I want to live the width of it as well." George did just that—he lived ninety-eight years while teaching others how they, too, could live the width of life.

Although you may have never heard of George Blair before picking up this book, you will be inspired by the way he lived, and you will be energized by his life lessons. Because of George's affinity for the number twenty-two, his birth date, this book is organized into twenty-two chapters.

So, without further ado, in the words of George Blair, let's "Do It."

George Alfred Blair was born at home in a rented duplex in Toledo, Ohio at 10:20 p.m., the third son of Roy Robert and Georgia (Gotshall) Blair. His brothers, Laurel and Robert (Bobby), were six and four years of age.

Georgia stayed home to raise the boys. Roy Robert became a successful banker and realtor, first working with partners, and later, as sole owner of The Blair Realty and Investment Company. He was a member of the Rotary Club, serving on many committees and as its director.

George's mother had her eye on a stately six-bedroom Colonial Revival home in what is now the historic Old West End and declared her intention to live there some day. When the house came up for sale, Roy Robert purchased it and moved his happy wife and children into the gracious home at 2055 Robinwood Avenue, Toledo, Ohio. The streets in this affluent neighborhood were paved with blocks of cedar wood to help muffle the sound of horses' hooves and carriage wheels.

In 1919, George's sister Betty was born. The family was complete. The Blair home was filled with laughter. Georgia and Roy Robert frequently entertained extended family and friends around the large dining room table. The Roaring Twenties were about to begin, and life was good.

As a young boy, George was close to his brother Bobby. Bobby was a clever child—he could build all kinds of ingenious devices. The two boys spent a lot of time testing out Bobby's ideas and creating prototypes.

But Bobby had asthma and was diagnosed with juvenile diabetes—during a time when insulin was just on the cusp of being discovered (1922). "Mother weighed his food, and at the table, he used saccharin out of a little bottle," young George wrote in an essay. "Many times, they took him a long way to a hospital. Once, when Grandmother was staying with us, we got a letter from Boston. Bobby had died." He was only eleven years old.

It was a sad time for the Blair family. The funeral was held in the living room. The house was filled with so many people that the minister had to stand on the landing of the staircase to give the sermon.

Years later, George wrote about this painful experience in a school essay:

> I was in Mother's room and we were all alone; she had me kneel down with her on the floor, and with an agonizing tenor-voiced appeal, she cried, 'Oh, God, our Bobby is up there with you someplace and I hope you are watching out for him. Be with our family and keep us together. Be with this boy of mine; keep him from all hurt, and forever on the straight and narrow path.' I loved my

mother very much. Do you suppose I could ever in my life let myself wander very far from the path she wanted me to travel?

Losing Bobby left a pain in seven-year-old George's heart. His older brother Laurel and his little sister Betty became more important to him. He also turned to his imagination and his fellow playmates for fun. The attic in the Robinwood home became a haven for his friends, a gang composed of Robin Hood, Captain Kidd (George's nickname), Jesse James, and other crusaders. Their signatures decorated the attic walls.

"I had virtually a national arsenal in the attic," George boasted of his youth. "My fancy broomstick sword had a large tin funnel for a guard, and my wood and leather decorated shield were the objects of envy of the rest of the gang. We had caves in vacant lots. Some were very intricate with two stories, long tunnels from one hidden entrance to the other side of the lot, and elaborate provisions against detection and attack. Our battles were mock affairs. We fought with swords and shield, and bows and arrows on garage roofs, tree tops, and retreating along in small dark passages between garages."

The attic became a workshop for a homemade ice boat that George and his friends crafted together. When it was finished, the boys faced a dilemma: How to get it out of the house?

The boat would not fit down the stairs. There was only one other way to get it out: through the attic window. George and his friends carefully lowered the boat to the ground with ropes. They spent many winters sailing on frozen Lake Erie at high speeds.

"I loved to ice skate. I was in Seventh Heaven when I was on racing blades. I would be out on the ice just stroking hard, going as fast as I could. It didn't matter how many friends I had along or no friends—I was just like a bird on the ice. Sometimes I would jump obstacles, like barrels. And sometimes I'd fall, and of course, it would always be on the base of my spine." It was because of back pain from the rough and tumble that George was seen by a doctor who noted that he had been born with a "marked scoliosis."

Roy Robert taught George to hunt when he was nine years old. When he turned eleven, his father's best friend gave George a shotgun. On the morning of opening day of hunting season, the men went out in the woods searching for game. During a lull in the activities, George wandered off on his own. In a large field of corn, he came close to a pheasant.

"I began the merry chase through the standing corn," George wrote in an essay. "I saw that the bird was heading for some brambles, so I crossed over a row and sprinted my fastest for seventy-five yards, crossed over four rows, and came up twenty-five feet behind him." George aimed and fired—and brought down his first pheasant. George's dog, Prince, picked up the scent, pounced on the bird, and brought it to George, dropping it proudly in his hands.

The group headed back to the house in good spirits at such a successful opening day. "Mr. Bayer broke my gun, emptied the magazine, and put it back together," George wrote. When they arrived home, Betty came to greet them. She wanted to see George's new gun, so he showed it to her.

"When I pulled the trigger, the magazine and chamber were supposed to be empty, but a ringing shot cut into the night air," George recalled. "For half an instant, the noise of the previous hustle and bustle of unloading and exchange of greetings was ghastly hushed."

George's mother let out a scream. Betty started sobbing. The bullet hit the cement driveway and Betty clutched her arm. Fortunately, the bullet ricocheted safely away and a grain of cement was the only thing that bounced off Betty's arm.

Chapter 2

Love in Bloom

GEORGE'S ENERGY WAS boundless. His mind was always racing with new ideas and innovative ways to become efficient. He explored the neighborhood thoroughly and calculated the quickest path to navigate to and from school. He had a deep thirst for learning—a skill that would serve him well throughout his life. George often visited the Toledo Museum of Art where his Uncle Ira served on the board of directors. Like his uncle, George had an avid interest in photography, so he spent many days in his uncle's basement, developing pictures in the darkroom.

Another uncle, Alfred George, married to Blanche, Georgia's sister, was a profound influence on George from an early age. His advice was, "Keep a pencil and pad beside your bed so that you can write down your ideas should you wake up in the middle of the night." Uncle A. G., as he was known, owned greenhouses raising flowers for the floral trade. He was a gifted painter and sculptor, as well.

Jack Sun became George's best friend. The two of them spent many hours together as Boy Scouts. "The Boy Scout movement devoured me. I was eager to learn everything and to win all the honors," George wrote. He rose quickly through the ranks, becoming senior patrol leader, camp bugler, and troop scribe.

He reflected about his parents, "I've got a swell Dad and a swell Mother. I wouldn't trade 'em for anything in the whole wide world. They never said, 'Don't do this or don't do that.' They just set a good example, offering a few words of advice, and they let me learn by the world's best teacher: experience. Dad was a good pal. His two pieces of advice which I'll never forget: 'Always be a gentleman,' and 'Use what you've got up here (as he pointed a finger to his head), that's what it's there for.'"

A Game of Patience

In one of his real estate development ventures, George's father created a housing subdivision and a golf course, which he named Heather Downs Country Club. George went to work for his dad, chopping down trees and clearing the woods. As the clubhouse was being built, George worked with the developers to create the greens around the two eighteen-hole courses. When it was completed, George played every hole over and over, sometimes playing each course twice in one day. Every time he hit a bad shot, he would strive to improve the next one.

"To me, it is the greatest game in the world," George said in 1934. "I used to have a quick, hot temper, but golf has taught me to master and control it."

To tamp down on his temper further, golf became his meditation. "I can walk the green, soft turf alone with nature and my thoughts," he said. George spent four years on the golf team in high school and was team captain for three of those years. (Later, his daughters would doubt that he lost his hot temper when he was young—since he still had it when he was a father!)

George's father, Roy Robert, was a wonderful role model. He taught George to network and serve in the community. "I liked the way my father was gregarious," George said in an interview. "He loved people the same way I do. He was free and easy; he loved to dance and play golf—he was a great golfer! He had all these professionals around him like Joe Kirkwood and Walter Hagen. Joe was the greatest trick artist of golfing, and Walter was the greatest golfer of his time. They were both guests of honor at our golf course. I got to know both of them, and it was good to be exposed to men of their caliber."

Music was another passion for George. Throughout his life, he played the drums, even drumming with his fork on a snack table when, near the end of his life, he could no longer speak. He started his own band and played the drums at Scott High School. Many Sundays, the band entertained at afternoon tea dances at Heather Downs Country Club.

"On Saturday nights during the Prohibition Era, we went out to Luna Pier, a large boardwalk on the outskirts of Toledo, a heavenly place in the summertime," George recalled. "We had all the big bands come to play on the boardwalk. One night, Cab Calloway was playing there and my friends urged me to play with him. At first, I was apprehensive, but eventually, they talked Cab into letting me sit in for one number. It was awesome! Amazingly enough, the same exact thing happened when Duke Ellington performed there!"

George occasionally hopped on empty boxcars as a form of transportation. He would later do a presentation on the tips and tricks to master riding the rails. On the way down to Florida for spring break, George shared a car with several hobos. Two of them ganged up on him when he refused to share a can of beans. They tossed George off the slow-moving train. He landed on his back and rolled down the embankment. Gradually and painfully, he stood up. He would have to catch the next train that slowed. This injury added to his future spinal problems.

One summer, George worked as an assistant purser on the *Tashmoo*. The boat sailed out of Detroit for day excursions on the St. Clair River during the week and moonlight cruises on the weekend.

On one of the trips, George noticed a young woman standing near the bow. She had an air of sophistication and self-confidence. Soft, wavy brown curls framed her face. Her hazel eyes, arching eyebrows, and elegant posture reminded George of the popular actress, Irene Dunne. The woman turned and smiled at George.

That's the girl I'm going to marry, he thought.

He had no idea who she was, but he simply knew he had to meet her.

Dorothy Eileen Spies was her name.

The end of summer came and George sent off his first letter to Dorothy, one of many more letters to come. He was smitten and very determined to get to know her. Soft-spoken yet tough, Dorothy was skilled in horse riding, fencing and archery. The two of them wrote long letters discussing their plans for college and their hopes for the future.

During his senior year at Scott High School, George focused on figuring out where he wanted to go to college. He had his heart set on attending Dartmouth, but a sudden change of economic circumstances derailed his plans. The Great Depression had set in, bringing the Roaring Twenties to an end. Almost overnight, the Blair family's finances plunged along with those of most of the population.

"I'm sorry, George; I can't afford to send you to Dartmouth," Roy Robert said.

George was disappointed, but he tried not to show it. He graduated from high school and went off to a public school, Miami University in Oxford, Ohio, where he studied government administration. He was determined to make the best of his time at Miami University. George joined the Delta Upsilon fraternity, and he spent a lot of time networking with other students. In between his heavy social life and school work, George continued to write letters to Dorothy, who was studying English at Wayne State University in Detroit.

Dorothy was a pretty and popular co-ed who was elected queen of Wayne's homecoming ceremonies. She won the school oratorical championship and went on to compete in the Michigan Intercollegiate Speech League competition. In March 1937, as Dorothy stepped up to the platform to deliver her speech, she had a heavy heart. Unknown to the contest officials, Dorothy's mother, Ruby, was dying of breast cancer. Immediately after her speech, Dorothy took off for the hospital without waiting for the results of the competition. (She won third place.)

George drove up from Ohio and met Dorothy and her family at the hospital. At four the next morning, Ruby passed away. As George stood by Dorothy's side at the funeral, their commitment to each other grew stronger. Although both were focused on their college classes, their letters to each other became more frequent and tender. He cherished receiving her letters and saved all of them.

George left Miami University in his junior year to work at the Citizens Survey Committee in Toledo. He enrolled in night classes at the University of Toledo. He left college to become the executive director of the United Citizens Council in Chicago. When that project came to an end, George became a research assistant to the editor of *American City* magazine in New York City. He drove his 1935 Ford Tudor to New York City and stayed at the Delta Upsilon house. He worked during the day and took courses at night at New York University.

George pursued yet another opportunity when he became executive secretary at the Pennsylvania Economy League in Pittsburgh. The Pennsylvania Economy League was founded during the Great Depression as a nonpartisan, public policy think tank for local and state government with offices in several large Pennsylvania cities. George was there for eleven months and then was transferred to the branch in Butler, Pennsylvania. He was fulfilling his passion for becoming a city planner.

There was rarely any "down" time for George. Naturally high in energy, he filled his days with as many different opportunities as he could fit in. He was a master at networking and bringing people together. He loved to write; he kept detailed journals and letters and documented much of his life. In his 1936 diary, George wrote:

> **9/6/1936 Sunday** Up at 8:30. To "Shack" [his family's Lake Erie house]—stopped at C. Foote's house. Met Dorothy, Don [her brother], Mr. and Mrs. Spies in Monroe at 1 p.m. The Spies drove out and met my family. Had swell dinner and then Dorothy and I took the boat out for a sail. Supper and cards until 8:30. Dorothy and I went to Toledo Beach for elegant dancing. Bed at 12:30 a.m.

George and Dorothy continued to write letters back and forth as the months went by. George dated other girls, but Dorothy was always on his mind. No one else could hold his attention the way Dorothy could. The physical distance between them was daunting—she was in Detroit and he was in New York City or Pennsylvania—but they saw each other on occasional weekends or school breaks. The feelings between them grew stronger and stronger.

On Thanksgiving night in 1938, he wrote this letter:

> Dorothy, my dear,
>
> On this once-a-year day dedicated to offering expressions of gratitude, my comparatively solitary existence has given ample time for thoughtful reflection. Already I have paid homage to my lovely mother and to my wonderful father. My thanks have gone up too for being alive, well, and happy. But there is yet another significant value for which I must give thanks—and that is our

friendship—as intolerable and limited as fate has fashioned it. All your snowy whiteness has unsurprisingly stood as a steadfast light to shine through foreboding fog and doubtful circumstances. You have been the source of inspiration for many people, so too, your influence has helped shape my finest ideals.

It has been my desire to offer you a tribute, and I have taken advantage of this particular day to do so.

May God continue to bless you and yours,
George

Another year went by and the two of them continued their long distant courtship. Now in her letters, Dorothy began to drop hints about marriage.

As Thanksgiving 1939 approached, George shared the news with his parents that he intended to ask Dorothy to marry him. His mother wrote to him, "Dorothy will be an ideal wife and companion. She will be a great help-mate for you and will grace any position. She is clever and a perfect dear." His grandmother (Rose Gotshall) wrote him a letter suggesting that he propose to Dorothy at the dinner table. "It may be the only request I ever make of you, so will you make me happy?"

That Thanksgiving, the family gathered around the dinner table. George's aunt stood up and said, "I have a Thanksgiving poem I'd like to read to you."

Thanksgiving Jingle Nov 23, 1939

Once upon a time as the story goes
A boy meets a girl on a summer cruise.

This lass was so dainty and so sweet
The lad thought her extremely neat.

So filled was she with art and grace
He knew she'd shine in any place.

This bright maid with her winning ways
Would surely make him happy days.

He surely thought he had found a pearl
She was so unlike any other girl.

This chap so handsome and so fine
Certainly had a convincing line.

This man of her dreams had now come true
For the likes of him were all too few.

He had travelled the country far and wide
To find this one girl to be his bride.

And now my friends we find it time
To hear the sequel to this rhyme.

As the family applauded, George stood up and turned to Dorothy. He unfolded a piece of paper and began to read to her:

> Thanksgiving days have usually been occasions of real thankfulness for me. It was on November 23 that Dorothy's mother, Ruby, was born (1886). It was on Thanksgiving Day thirty-one years ago [1908] that my mother and father announced their intentions to marry. And now, on this Thanksgiving, I pray that your father will announce to our families and to the world that you will accept my proposal for a lifelong union.
>
> We are young enough to have the world before us, and yet we are old enough to know that the world is not at our feet.
>
> If your heart, mind, body, and soul are unalterably desirous of uniting with me then as a sacred token of our mutual faith, I should like you to wear this ring forever.

Dorothy was radiant. With graceful composure, she accepted. He slipped the diamond ring onto her slender finger.

On December 30, George, his best man, Jack Sun, and several of his groomsmen left Toledo in George's car heading for Detroit at eleven in the morning. The wedding was set for 4 p.m. at St. Paul's Episcopal Cathedral. Christmas greens, swags of holly, and poinsettias decorated the altar.

With her attendants, Dorothy walked down the aisle in a lovely ivory moiré gown with a sweetheart neckline and a fingertip veil secured to a halo of lace trimmed with orange blossoms. She carried a bouquet of white orchids and a white prayer book. George in morning tailcoat and striped trousers, standing next to Jack, watched with pride as Dorothy came closer. Just as he predicted when he first laid eyes on her, the girl on the ship was now becoming his wife.

After the Honeymoon

Their honeymoon was a whirlwind road trip, including Philadelphia and New York City, where George showed Dorothy all the sights and glamour. Their last stop was a bucolic resort in the Poconos. After the honeymoon, they settled in Butler, Pennsylvania, where George continued to work as the executive secretary of the Pennsylvania Economy League. He also worked for the Chamber of Commerce as a special surveyor for industrial businesses. For four years, he put his analytical skills to work and was instrumental in saving taxpayers over one million dollars. George enrolled in night classes, this time at Carnegie Institute of Technology and the University of Pittsburgh. He taught a course in elementary corporation accounting at Pennsylvania State College in Butler.

They enjoyed a full social life. Dorothy had previously taught dance at the Arthur Murray studio in Detroit. She and George loved to dance, and they spent many weekends at balls and parties. George often paid the price the next morning, for his back pain made it difficult to get out of bed. Once he was up and moving about, he seemed to be better. However, he knew he couldn't let his back problems stop him from living his life—especially when he was about to become a father.

Chapter 3

Becoming a Dad

The Blairs' first child, Donna Laurel, was born in October 1941. It was no secret that George was hoping for a boy, so they chose to name her after Dorothy's brother Donald and George's brother Laurel.

With World War II unfolding, George wanted to serve his country, but he was denied enlistment because of his chronic back condition. Instead, he served as a Junior Administrative Officer with the US Army Air Corps in the Cost Analysis Branch at the Wright Patterson Air Force Base. He analyzed costs of contractors for procurements.

As the country mobilized to support the war effort, one of his assignments in 1943 took him to the Ford Motor Plant in Detroit that was tooling up for war production. While he was there, he noticed a disturbing trend among the workers: They were using work time to play games, talk, and lounge. The guys who were hauling parts between the plants often left the trucks running for hours at a time, and many of them carried half-empty loads. Jobs that should have taken days to complete stretched out for weeks.

After several months of observing inefficient procedures and wasted time, George penned a letter to the War Production Board in Washington, DC, offering suggestions for how to improve their services nationwide.

"Morale is at a low ebb," George wrote. "Each man should have his job explained to him so that he feels he isn't only drawing a paycheck, but is really accomplishing something of great importance. This gives a man an incentive and a goal."

George suggested implementing morning pep talks, upbeat music and songs, and positive words and posters to change the morale and increase production. "A daily routine becomes stagnant, but a new outlook can be obtained if a goal is pointed out."

And finally, in the name of efficiency, George suggested that his own job could be run by a much lower paid employee to cut costs.

George and Dorothy welcomed their second daughter, Georgia Rose, in April 1945. Again, George was hoping for a son to take his name, so his new little girl was named both for him and his mother, Georgia. They nicknamed her GeeGee.

Shortly after, George was transferred to the Watson Laboratories in New Jersey. The Blairs settled in a red brick Tudor home on a circular street, Buttonwood Drive, a tranquil neighborhood lined with shade trees and sturdy homes. Shrewsbury was a charming small town where the children could walk or ride their bicycles to school and to the tiny post office in the middle of Sycamore Avenue. There were two historic churches and a Quaker Meeting house in the center of town. The bell in the clock tower at the Episcopal church marked the time of day.

In April 1948, a third daughter was born. She was named Carrie Elizabeth, after two favorite aunts. She was nicknamed CB.

Lastly, in May 1950, their fourth daughter, Dorothy Roberta, was born. Named after her mother and grandfather, she was nicknamed Robin.

Family Sports

There was no shortage of fun in the Blair household. The family often spent winter weekends ice skating and ice boating on the Navesink River in Red Bank. Following his childhood interest in ice boating, George became the Commodore of the North Shrewsbury Ice Boat and Yacht Club, the oldest continuously operating club in the world. He competed in the Arrow class sailing his "Death Trap," "Yellow Fever," and "Yellow Trouble" ice boats. This sport was perfect for George because it is fast and requires precision. You can sail faster than the wind. Trimming the sails makes the wind flow over them, creating lift, much like an airplane wing. The boats often reach speeds of 60 to 100 mph.

Having grown up in Ohio and Michigan, winter sports were second nature to George and Dorothy. George took great delight in lining up his four daughters on the ice and jumping over them on his racing skates. "It would seem scary to onlookers, but the four of us had total confidence in our father's ability to leap over us," GeeGee recalled. On windy days, George rigged an ice wing and skated down the river at breakneck speeds. Dorothy used a skate sail to keep up. She never traded in her black hockey skates from college days for figure skates.

Back home on Buttonwood Drive, after a snowstorm dumped several inches of snow, George tied a ski rope to the boat hitch on the back of his Cadillac, and in a flash, the neighborhood kids would show up, clamoring for a ride behind the car on skis or a sled.

The family sometimes headed to New England, New York or Pennsylvania to snow ski. George wasn't content to ski on ordinary skis. Instead, he preferred Shortee skis (36") or barrel staves. The short, curved pieces from an old barrel allowed for 360-degree turns and some creative skiing.

"Daddy would ski doing continuous turns down the mountain," Carrie recalled. "He could sit down on a mogul and do a forward somersault and come up skiing."

The younger skiers often stared at George with his strange skis. An older guy on short skis—they figured he would be the slowest one down the mountain.

They were wrong.

George always loved a challenge. As soon as a young skier would take off, George would power after him. He would zoom by him effortlessly, leaving him in his wake with a stunned look on his face.

On spring weekends, George and Dorothy often rode their tandem bike with several other couples. They formed a group called the Big Wheels, and they planned day trips around town. As secretary of the Big Wheel Club, Dorothy jokingly presented to George an honorary "Doctorate of Big Wheel" degree during one of their meetings.

For years, the Blairs organized a Fourth of July parade. Dorothy cleverly sewed the costumes. Donna dressed as the Statue of Liberty, and GeeGee acted as the majorette, twirling a baton. Carrie, Robin, and the neighborhood children dressed up as soldiers or nurses, complete with "bloody" bandages and crutches, and several marched while beating drums and playing kazoos.

"All the kids in the neighborhood would participate," Robin recalled. "Parents would stand at the curb, cheering, clapping, and waving the American flag."

On the Fourth of July in 1950, GeeGee, five years old, flew by herself, to Toledo to visit her grandmother. George insisted she could not go unless she learned to tie her shoelaces. He did not want his elderly mother to lean over to help his little girl. So he practiced with her until she could tie the laces on her own. One of his philosophies was that a parent's job is to instill independence in his or her children. GeeGee enjoyed the plane trip by herself, especially because she could watch the fireworks going on below.

CHAPTER 4

The Birth of an Entrepreneur

GEORGE AND DOROTHY's young married life was influenced by the belt-tightening years of World War II. Their four daughters were born between 1941 and 1950. When the United States finally shook free of the strife of war, the economy began to grow at a great rate. George's timing in the twentieth century was both difficult and fortunate. He wanted to work for himself so kept alert to find a need he could fill. He quickly and cleverly learned how to balance risk-taking with secure investments, building many businesses from scratch with good ideas, impeccable planning, and dedicated employees. He had boundless self-confidence and a willingness to experiment. Like his father, he knew the economy could fluctuate, and he learned his lessons well. He faithfully saved, purchased only what he could afford, and shunned the early "buy on credit/layaway" plans that got many people into trouble. His philosophy was to pay cash, "Don't owe the bank. Play games of skill, not chance." His entrepreneurial spirit eventually paid him back handsomely.

Fogging Unlimited 1948

George's idea for his first business, Fogging Unlimited, came from an unlikely place: the *Better Homes and Gardens* magazine. One article featured a new process of fogging to target insects in hard-to-reach places. George grabbed a magnifying glass to read the name of the company displayed on a truck: Todd Shipyards of Brooklyn, New York. He contacted the company and arranged for a representative to come to his home and demonstrate the new product.

The fog machine was originally made for the Navy to put on ship sterns. The machine created a fog so thick that it hid the ship from sight. One of the Navy crewmen had the brilliant idea to drop a little insecticide into one of the machines to keep the mosquitoes off the ship.

At the time, New Jersey led the nation in mosquito-control programs, which began in 1912. George saw this new fogging method as an opportunity to help reduce the outbreak of encephalitis rampant in the area. He purchased a truck, outfitted it with the fogging equipment, and recruited his first employee. Fogging Unlimited was in business.

Hospital Picture Service 1949

George had no idea that his life was about to change yet again when he stepped into the Watson Laboratory infirmary to seek treatment for a sore throat. While he was sitting in the waiting room, he picked up a copy of *RN Magazine* and absentmindedly browsed through it. An article on photography caught his eye. Robert Clark of Washington, DC was taking pictures of newborn babies in a Virginia hospital and selling copies to the parents. The idea of taking pictures of newborn babies was a novel one. Few families had cameras to take pictures of their babies. The Blairs were fortunate—George was a photographer so he had taken pictures of his children soon after they were born.

George was inspired. Thousands of hospitals were spread across the country—what if there was a way to automate the process and get every hospital to provide this service? He went home and immediately wrote a letter to Robert Clark. Weeks went by, without any response.

Undaunted, George found Clark's phone number and called him. Clark invited him to see his 100-pound camera and observe the photographing process. George wasted no time. The next day, he got in his car and drove to Virginia.

Robert showed George the prototype: an aircraft-mapping camera mounted to an awkward wooden platform with a baby scale underneath. It was heavy, bulky, and difficult to move, but it was operational.

On the ride home, George's mind began to race as different ideas flowed to him. He was going to create a better, smaller camera using 120mm film. He would offer a complete service to local hospitals. George selected a straightforward name for his business: Hospital Picture Service (HPS). Later, he took pictures of his youngest daughter, Robin, who became a frequent model for his marketing materials.

George's vision was simple: create an integrated system. It would include a rolling supply cabinet with a curved tray on which to place the baby securely. The automatic camera was positioned on a post above the tray. A foot switch activated the shutter to take the picture. It would be easily operated by nurses and auxiliary volunteers. George imagined the parents' joy when they viewed their newborns' portraits.

George signed up his first hospital: Middlesex General Hospital, housed in an old-fashioned red brick building in New Brunswick, New Jersey. "It was a cold, snowy afternoon, and I fought the wind as I carefully wheeled the very first HPS camera up a back ramp," George recalled. Even though this was the first hospital he signed a contract with, George knew there was one way he could truly stand out: provide high quality and value. The pictures were taken on the baby's first day before 3 p.m. The film was mailed to the processing lab, set up in the basement of George's house. In a rapid turnaround unheard of in the '50s, the black-and-white film was developed, and the pictures printed, packed, and mailed back to the hospital the very next day.

Now that he had his first hospital, George hit the road and visited one hospital after another. Sometimes he was gone for days, leaving Dorothy at home with the four girls. Money was tight because George was no longer working at Watson Laboratories. He was juggling two start-up businesses that took all his capital. Dorothy found frugal ways to make every dollar stretch. To nurture the artist within her, she created "DEBware." The name was created from her initials **D**orothy **E**ileen **B**lair. Her special-order commemorative plates were painted in gold and fired in her home ceramic studio. The local china and glass shops would often refer clients to her when they needed personalized graphics and wording to celebrate anniversaries, birthdays, and other special occasions. Dorothy's daughters still cherish her lovely script painted on the birth announcement plates she made for each of them.

Donna, the oldest daughter, recalled, "I thought we were poor. We didn't have new furniture in our house. My younger sisters all wore mostly hand-me-down shoes. My dad drove used cars, and my mom did not have a car; she had groceries delivered or walked to the store. My grandmother finally handed down her car to my mother. People had this view that Dad was a lot richer than he really was—my father worked very hard. He always presented himself with confidence."

The hospital picture business expanded rapidly, so George had to borrow money to purchase the cameras and hire staff. George was running both businesses from the basement in his home in Shrewsbury. There was little privacy for Dorothy and the children with the growing number of employees needing access to the house.

Without the security of a full-time job with benefits, George worked obsessively. When he was on the road, he made the most of his time by continuing to network with as many people as he could, and he kept each contact in a black address book with notes.

George's intense, gregarious attitude made almost every hospital director say "yes" to the baby picture business during the first sales appointment. George made sure to point out the mutual benefits of the service—a keepsake that every family would treasure as well as extra money for the hospital. It was a business deal that was a win-win on both sides—and for the families as well. At the end of his first year, George had twelve hospitals signed up. By the second year, he had twenty.

Taskmaster

By 1954, the hospital picture business grew so large that George had to move it out of the family home. He purchased a building in Red Bank at 28 Linden Place and hired more employees. To save time and money at Hospital Picture Service, George studied the whole process of his photo business and devised ways to streamline every aspect of it. The "plant" was a long room with a Formica counter the entire length of one wall. High windows let in abundant light. The baby pictures were packed by employees sitting in a row at this counter. Each had a station with the supplies needed. It was an efficient production line. As George purchased surrounding residential properties, it expanded into a small complex of offices.

"Mr. Blair wanted his employees to feel like family," said Kathy Wolcott, the production manager. For their use, the kitchen/break room was stocked with popcorn, milk, butter, whole grain bread, and bananas—but no coffee. He felt that coffee was not healthy, so he never drank it. There was a coffee maker, but the employees had to supply their own coffee. Everyone looked forward to the annual holiday parties, and all employees received a day off on their birthdays, with pay. Employees got to enjoy many other perks, such as the use of the company cars. George also provided medical and dental insurance. This was a generous policy, much more so than the average small employer. His personal dentist was available to his employees for routine preventative care without charge to them.

From a young age, George's four daughters worked at HPS, sometimes even at night. "We sat at the counter and did 'rejects,' sorting through the photo packages that were returned from the hospital," Carrie recalled. "Daddy had us race with each other, and we quickly learned how to line up the envelopes in a certain way, pull the elements apart, and arrange the reusable paper in different piles, so that it would be recycled."

Robin remembers, "We didn't think of it as work; we made it into a contest. We had rolling chair races, played hide-and-seek in the film processing dark rooms, and would play in the large cardboard shipping boxes."

Hospital Picture Service was structured as a family business so George could teach his daughters core business values and shared goals as a family. George instilled a solid work ethic in each girl and had high expectations for all of them. All four daughters eventually worked for the family businesses.

George's expectations of others became a lesson to them and later shaped George's famous motto: Do It. (His slogan was a part of him long before Nike's "Just Do It.") "There was no such word as 'can't' in George's dictionary," GeeGee explained. "He believed if you wanted to do something—go do it. Don't hesitate; just figure it out." Another word that was not used in the Blair house was "bored."

"Mr. Blair had his own system of shorthand," said Nick Mazza, technical director of camera production at HPS. "PSM meant 'Please see me.'" Each employee was required to keep a notepad near the phone and to record as much information as possible for transactions. Another shorthand notation was LM which meant "Left a message."

"Whenever my dad talked to someone, he would take notes," GeeGee recalled. "I have some of the notes he wrote when he talked to me. You had to be careful what you said because you knew he was writing it down. He also did not like twisted phone cords. We all learned to disconnect the cords to let them unwind, then plug them back in. If he stopped at your desk, he would unwind it himself if your cord was not straight."

George taught his employees that "The customer is always right. When you are taking a call from a customer, do whatever it takes to satisfy his needs." Kathy Baily, the office manager said, "He wanted things to be done right the first time. It showed that we cared about the business and about quality."

George was demanding but nurturing from a business standpoint. He looked for a person's potential and figured out how to encourage it. Dorothy's housekeeper, Lorese Wilson, had a spark that George recognized. When he purchased an IBM main frame computer for HPS, he asked Lorese whether she would like to learn how to do data entry. She was anxious for advancement, and this opportunity launched her into a new career in the computer department.

After college, GeeGee went to work at HPS full-time. "One of my jobs was buying supplies," GeeGee later recalled. "Dad wanted me to get the highest quality—but at the lowest price. I'd call and negotiate. If I could get it for twenty, he would say, 'Can you get it for eighteen? You never know how low low is.' You have to keep asking for the best price. So I would call back and try for a lower price." George was meticulous about quality—he created marketing materials that displayed the same quality as the photographs they sold. "Our stationery was very heavy, beautiful paper with gold embossing so when someone picked it up, the person knew it was an important letter," GeeGee said.

Blair Motion Bassinet

During his visits to various hospitals, George noticed a lot of babies were crying and there simply weren't enough nurses to attend to each newborn. George had an idea: What if he could find a way to make the bassinet move so the rhythmic motion could soothe a baby?

George put together a prototype and leased it to a hospital. He offered a free thirty-day trial. The nurses were enthusiastic about the new Blair Motion Bassinet. The frame George manufactured was the same size as a nursey bassinet, but the base had a motor attached and a mechanism on which the bassinet could slide gently back and forth. "The Blair Motion Bassinet helps to calm our irritable infants, and quiets the babies of drug-addicted mothers. It also helps save a nurse from continually rocking a sick baby," said Karen Grant, RN, Boston. The same concept became popular when vibrating infant seats and cribs were common paraphernalia to soothe babies at home.

George was a taskmaster at home. "Learning to ride a two-wheel bicycle was an act of faith when Daddy taught us," said GeeGee. "Training wheels were not allowed. He put you on the bike, held onto the back of the seat while you got your balance, and then let you go on your own with the words, 'You can do it! I know you can do it!' You believed you could because he told you that you could."

"He was tough," Robin explained. "He had high expectations and he wanted us to be efficient. I was not a particularly good student; I didn't apply myself. I liked school for the social aspect—I had fun and I was popular with my classmates, and most of my teachers liked me, despite my just average grades. That was a problem with my dad. He tried tutoring me in math, but he was so strict that I just crumbled under the pressure. Tutoring didn't last long. Dad loved numbers, statistics, and charting things. I loved art and music. He later understood my focus on the arts."

GeeGee's best friend, Lori Lyons, was an only child. She delighted in being at the Blair house because there were four sisters and lots of commotion. When they were about ten years old, the girls had a sleepover. Lori recalls, "After we were all in our pajamas and ready to go to bed, suddenly Mr. Blair called a fire drill. We rushed into the second-floor master bedroom. He attached a rope ladder under the sill and flung it out the window. He supervised as each person climbed down the wobbly ladder in the dark. It was scary and thrilling. You didn't say 'no' when Mr. Blair told you to do something."

Perhaps George's constant back pain made him particularly demanding, but it also meant there was never a dull minute in the Blair home.

Chapter 5

A Barefoot Water Skier Is Born

GEORGE'S BACK PROBLEMS became increasingly worse. The only way he could get out of bed was to roll out and land on the floor on his hands and knees. He gradually, and oh-so-slowly, worked his way up into a standing position by crawling his hands up a wall. Once he was up and did some stretches, he regained his mobility and moved on with his day. The pain was often compounded if George remained seated too long.

No rhyme or reason could be found for when his back would give out or the pain would flare up. George visited two local doctors, whose advice was the same: take it easy and no heavy lifting.

One afternoon, George and Dorothy were at an auction where they won the bid on a beautiful, upholstered chair. As George was lifting the chair into the car, his back gave out. He suffered excruciating pain. There was no way he could continue to suffer like that. He made an appointment with an osteopathic doctor who ordered x-rays.

Five different doctors reviewed George's case. They asked him to list all the incidents leading up to his back problems.

"I have had the ordinary run of accidents and falls that any normal active boy would have and maybe a few more," George explained. "I was the outstanding athlete of my grade school, and I was runner-up for the State Championship (50-yard dash, broad jump, high jump, etc.) in Toledo. I fell off a freight train in 1934. In the winters of '41 and '42, I did a lot of ice skating and prided myself on the number of barrels I could jump, but of course, several times I landed squarely on the bottom of my spine."

Finally, after seeing multiple doctors, George had a formal diagnosis: spondylolisthesis, a condition in which part of the spine is displaced, with one vertebra slipping forward over another. Two of the doctors gave George an osteopathic treatment and recommended weekly, ongoing therapy to see whether his back condition would improve.

If there was no improvement, one option remained: spinal surgery with a 50/50 chance of success. George declined. He wasn't ready to face an operation that, if it weren't successful, could leave him permanently in a wheelchair. He tried sleeping flat on his back with a board under his mattress to ease the pain.

For the next nine years, George continued to work hard on expanding his two businesses and raising his daughters. Both he and Dorothy were active in the Shrewsbury community. Dorothy enrolled all of the girls in the Girl Scouts. In 1924, when Dorothy was nine years old, she met the founder of Girl Scouting, Juliette Low, who inspired her to earn the Golden Eaglet in 1933. She became a troop leader for her daughters, then a director of the Monmouth Council of Girl Scouts, staying involved with scouting for over sixty-five years.

As the years went by, George's back problems escalated so he began to withdraw from physical activity. Finally, in 1953, George reached the point where he could no longer function well throughout the day. His new doctor, Anthony J. Pisani, the orthopedic surgeon for the New York Giants football team, urged him to consider the spinal fusion surgery. George finally consented, despite the possibility of ending up in a wheelchair if the surgery was unsuccessful. His pain was unrelenting.

Fortunately, the surgery at St. Vincent's Hospital in New York City went well. Afterwards, George transferred to a rehabilitation facility for a few weeks. Once back home, he wore a stiff brace and spent several more weeks in bed. The girls all took turns caring for him, massaging his arms and back as he healed. "My dad had a pair of 'upside down' glasses that allowed him to read lying flat in bed," Robin recalled. The whole family pitched in to keep the businesses running as George recuperated.

George's back had mended well under the stiff leather brace. His doctor now suggested that he go somewhere warm to help his rehabilitation.

"Let's go to Florida with the girls," George told Dorothy. So they piled into the car and headed to Fort Lauderdale, making several stops along the way to visit hospitals for the baby picture business. Combining business with fun allowed George to reap tax benefits for his business while he worked to expand to more hospitals. But the trips to Florida also gave the family a chance to visit with the girls' grandparents, Roy and Georgia Blair, who were "snowbirds" from Ohio.

On one of these trips, George was sitting on a bench taking a break from a walk along the Intracoastal Waterway when he noticed some water skiers zipping by. The instructor, Lyle Lee, was teaching the group. George was intrigued as he sat there and watched.

"Hey, don't you want to join the fun?" Lyle asked, coming up to George and pointing to the water.

"No, no, I can't. I'm too old, and I've had a terrible operation on my back," George said. He pointed to the leather brace strapped around his chest.

"Well, can you walk?"

"Well, yeah; I walked over here, didn't I?"

"If you can walk, you can water ski. Come on; let's give it a try."

George, always up for a challenge, got into the water, and Lyle helped him put his feet in the bindings. He instructed George to hold on to the boom—a metal bar 6-8' long that extends out from either side of a ski boat and is angled slightly forward. A cable system at the end of the boom is attached to the bow eye hook (front of the boat) for support. It gives the skier a solid hold especially for learning, instead of the 75' towline behind the boat.

"Keep your knees bent, arms straight, and let the boat do the work," Lyle instructed.

George did as he was told. He rose out of the water and turned to look at Lyle with a huge smile on his face.

"The first time I got up on skis, I felt like a giant weight had been lifted from my mind and my body. I loved it so much because for all those years I was always worried about my health, and suddenly I felt great," George told a reporter from the *Tampa Tribune* in 1989.

"I was so happy to do something athletic. It was like I was reborn."

Now George wanted the whole family to learn to water ski. By the end of the week, all six of the Blairs got up on skis behind the boat at the same time.

In keeping with George's fascination with photographs, the Blairs had a tradition of sending out a family photo greeting card for Christmas. In 1958, the photo was of the six Blairs water skiing at one time, dressed in matching bathing suits. Robin was just seven years old.

At the end of their vacation, George purchased a boat and trailer from Lyle. As they drove back home with the boat in tow, George was beyond excited. The new sport had quickly become his passion. Water skiing gave him a thrill he had never experienced before.

When George returned to Shrewsbury, he wanted to share the sport with others. The whole family spent their weekends on the water, going from two skis to one. George began buying all kinds of skis—trick skis, swivel skis, shoe skis, and slalom skis. He even had a disk made of plywood (a 36" round flat board) used for doing tricks. The disk can rotate in all directions if the skier is skillful.

In true entrepreneurial fashion, George created another business in 1957: Family Ski School. The first school was located on the Navesink River in Red Bank, New Jersey. Later, George opened a second ski school in Edison, New Jersey, on Mirror Lake. George loved to end every lesson by heading back to the dock at full speed; he would deftly pull back on the throttle and gracefully glide in at the last moment. He insisted that his young daughters drive in this fashion as well. Carrie recalls, "Daddy wanted the throttle wide open, pressed full forward, going as fast as the 100-hp Mercury outboard would go. We were not allowed to slow down as we approached the dock. We had to wait until it seemed we would crash before pulling the throttle all the way back quickly to neutral, whereupon, the boat coasted, settled down into the water, and floated gently to the dock. This scared everyone in the boat and everyone watching. But he had perfect timing and just needed you to get perfect timing, too. It demonstrated his risk-taking and thrill-seeking while calculating everything to within a hair's breadth of danger. I trusted him implicitly and never knew him to make a mistake that endangered anyone. He was a big showoff, too."

George guaranteed that he could teach anyone to ski. His absolute faith in himself and his inability to accept failure gave hundreds of new skiers a positive boost and lots of fun. He created an efficient formula for getting the skier up and smiling, using the boom, and instructing the skier while driving the boat. He exuded confidence. If a quiet explanation did not get results, some intimidation and scolding did. He was convincing and always ready to celebrate his students' achievements.

Skiing was truly a family affair. The Blairs joined the local ski club, the Jersey Ski-Ters, in 1962. They also had their own ski shows as well as doing shows with the club. Dorothy was the ski show announcer. Gee-Gee twirled a baton while on skis. Carrie donned a clown suit. Robin was a ballerina, performing gracefully on a slalom ski while in a toe-hold or climbing the skiers' pyramids. Like their dad, the girls loved skiing and teaching the sport to others. Driving the boat was a thrill, and they excelled at it, becoming precision drivers.

"We stayed out on the water every night until dark and the mosquitoes drove us in," Carrie recalled. "We hosed down the equipment; put away the life preservers, ropes, handles, skis, and gas cans; and then we'd count the money."

Turning his passion for water skiing into a business was a brilliant move for George. He purchased a motorcycle/scooter business in 1957 that he called Scotch Scooters (due to his Scottish heritage). In 1960, he expanded it to include a boat business. He combined them into a new store in Red Bank called The Boat, Ski, and Scooter Center.

The business allowed George to purchase boats, equipment, and fuel—while realizing the tax benefits of a small business. George employed a mechanic, Ben Hover, who kept the fleet of HPS company cars and vans, plus the boats and motors in top running order.

In June of 1958, George was sitting in his office reflecting on the positive changes in his life. He recognized that his spinal fusion had given him the opportunity to discover a sport that had opened a whole new world to him. He was so moved with gratitude that he called in his secretary, Ruth, and dictated a letter to his surgeon:

Dr. A.J. Pisani,

Five years ago today, you performed a fusion with a rib bone from another patient to correct my marked spondylolisthesis. The diagnosis of my trouble had been made as early as 1942. For eleven years, I steadfastly resisted having surgery, fearing the operation itself and doubting the outcome.

Even though I had sadly given up golfing, snow skiing, ice skating, gardening, and any pastime requiring over twenty pounds of lifting, pulling, or pushing, my condition gradually deteriorated. For many years, I couldn't sleep on my back without my legs becoming numb. Early in the day, I couldn't even bend over to wash my face. The most terrifying, though, were trips away from home. I remember, oh too well, the sleepless night on the floor at the Stevens Hotel in Chicago; the torturous night in Scarsdale when by 3:00 a.m. I packed up and left; the night in a Washington, D.C. hotel when the pain was so unbearable I couldn't sleep in the bed or on the floor or sitting up, and when morning finally came, I was doubtful I could shuffle to the elevator and quite sure I'd never be able to drive home.

Well, only ten days following the operation in St. Vincent's hospital in New York City, you transferred me by ambulance to Riverview Hospital in Red Bank for another ten days. Then I came home and walked upstairs! Six months later, I was gingerly splashing in a swimming pool and today—even at the ripe old age of forty-three—I dance all evening, scuba dive, play eighteen holes of golf, ride ten miles on a tandem bicycle, and do tricks on water skis better than any of our four agile children.

You, and the good Lord, have made me a happy man out of a sorry specimen. I am, therefore, sending you this unsolicited testimonial already framed in the hope that you will show it to at least one "doubting Thomas" who needlessly procrastinates his cure under your skillful care.

I shall never be able to adequately repay you.

Sincerely yours,
George A. Blair

Learning to Barefoot

Six years after learning to water ski, George was yearning for more. At this point, he had collected several medals from competing in water ski tournaments. There was one thing on his bucket list that he simply had to learn: barefoot water skiing. "I saw a guy barefooting," George recalled, "and I thought, 'Now that's a real challenge!' It looked so impossible to me that I had to try it." George called Leo Bentz at Lee's Ski School in North Miami Beach. Leo was the man who designed and manufactured the Ski Nautique line of boats.

"Do you think you can teach an old man to barefoot?" George asked him.

"If you've got the will, I'll show you how," Leo said.

The ski school was located on a stretch of water that was calm 90 percent of the time. Leo had no boom on his boat, so George had to learn on a long line behind the boat. Leo handed him a ski—it was nothing more than a simple board without a binding on it.

"Go outside the wake, put your foot in the water, and put more and more pressure on it until you can put your other foot in the water," Leo instructed.

George spent the first two days hitting the hard water face first. By the third day, he was tired and bruised, his feet burned, and his body ached all over. He was frustrated, but there was just no way he was going to give up and go home defeated.

On the third day, George emerged triumphant: He finally barefoot water skied!

Looking back on those three tough days, George recalled the frustration he felt. "There are certain plateaus you have in every sport and that was certainly one of mine."

George had no idea how much taking up a new aspect of water skiing would change the course of his life. From that day on, barefooting became his ultimate passion on the water.

"Just plain water skiing, now that's a high for most people. And I remember the first time I could ski on one ski—that was one of my biggest highs. Then there was the first time I did a standing-dock start on one ski—I remember that high very distinctively. But barefooting is still the highest high of all," said George.

Early in the morning, George would get out of bed and head out to the boat. "He would barefoot for three miles on the Navesink River, starting at the dock in Red Bank and ending at the bridge," Gene Quigley, one of his drivers and a ski team member, recalled. "I never really saw him in a bad mood. I have a physical disability myself—and George taught me to achieve things I never would have done without his encouragement and expertise."

George expanded his ski show repertoire—performing on trick skis, a disk, a three-foot high stool, and hydrofoil skis to include his signature bare-footing move: no hands with rope-in-teeth. He was a stuntman at heart, creating his own repertoire of tricks. During a trip to Florida, George performed for the first time at the famous Cypress Gardens Ski Show. Cypress Gardens was like the Hollywood of the east, with beautiful gardens, swim performances, skating, music, all very glamorous.

Kite Flying on Skis

Ken Tibado of Lake Wales, Florida, introduced George to kite flying. The flat trapezoidal kites were fifteen feet long and twelve feet wide, tethered to the boat via a 110-foot line. George quickly became skilled at flying the kite and added it to the Jersey ski shows, always using it as the last act. "I feel as free as a bird up there!" George started off on two skis and rose into the air when the boat speed reached 28 mph. To be more dramatic, he would kick off the skis and do a barefoot landing. At shows ending at dusk, he would set off the flares attached to the kite, making it appear as if it were on fire.

"Ken taught me to fly the kite from a trapeze ten feet underneath it. As far as I know, we were the only two who did that, and that feat once got me into a jam," George told *The Water Skier* magazine.

George was appointed as assistant team manager to the US Water Ski Team. The team traveled to the World Championships in Australia. When the Australians learned that George could fly a kite with a trapeze, they begged for a demonstration.

George, in his haste, forgot to attach his safety release to the trapeze. "When the kite took off, there I was, dangling in the air hanging by my arms," George recalled. The crew quickly realized the mistake and landed George safely. He took off again, this time with the release in place.

Even though the flat kite was difficult to maneuver, all George's daughters learned to fly. Success depended not only on the skier but also on the skill of the boat driver and the wind. One gusty day on the Navesink River, George was out with Carrie and Robin (twelve and ten years old). It was Robin's turn. She took off and was happily soaring above the water. A sudden gust threw the kite into a wild gyration fifty feet above the water. She overcorrected and the pendulum swing got worse. She lost her skis.

George knew it would take precision driving and timing to get her down safely. Carrie was the "pin man," holding a short line to a quick release that would disconnect the kite towline from the boat. George warned her to pull the release *only* on his command. Carrie knew her sister could be seriously hurt if she didn't follow her Dad's instructions precisely. The pressure was intense.

George turned the boat into the wind. Robin, still out of control, descended closer to the water. He cut the throttle back, and at the last moment, he yelled, "Pull the pin!" seconds before Robin would have crashed and been dragged under the water.

The kite settled on the water. Robin unsnapped her harness from the kite, but another gust of wind flipped it back, tangling her in the tow rope. From the boat, George managed to grab a corner of the kite, now sinking, lifting it enough for Robin to free herself and swim to the boat. Finally, everyone could exhale in relief. This was before the Delta Wing kites became popular and replaced the flat kite in ski shows.

George decided to take airplane flying lessons in the mid-1960s. His friend, who was a United Airlines pilot, also taught private students at the small Red Bank Airport. GeeGee and Robin joined him for lessons. It was tricky flying a Cessna 150 in and out of an airport that had power and telephone lines at both ends of the east and west runway. But all three soloed within a few months. Later in Florida, George and Robin enjoyed flying a seaplane with an instructor.

The Hudson River Outboard Marathon 1963

The Hudson River Outboard Marathon, a 134-mile outboard race from Albany to New York City down the Hudson River, began in the 1920s. In 1963, George decided to enter the race despite having no racing experience. He asked eighteen-year-old GeeGee to be his co-driver.

"Sometimes I did things with Dad not because I really wanted to, but because I didn't want him to be sorry that he didn't have a son."

Their fifteen-foot Hydrodyne ski boat was outfitted with an 80-hp Mercury outboard. Of the eighty-nine boats that started the race, eighty-three finished. One boat lost a transom and one driver knocked out some front teeth.

"It was nothing but relentless, mind-blowing bouncing as we raced," GeeGee recalled. For three hours and fifteen minutes, the boat pounded along at an average speed of 44.5 mph. George and GeeGee took turns driving and switched fuel tanks without stopping. The river was relatively smooth until the last twenty-five miles, when the wind and rolling wakes from freighters tested their endurance as they headed toward the finish line near 79th Street Marina in New York City. They came in first in their Class H division.

When it came to racing, Donna and Robin participated in water ski endurance races. In one particular race, the LeMans Marathon, Donna faced a twenty-mile ski run in 36° weather with high winds and whitecaps. She came in third. One contestant was treated for hypothermia. In the annual Aquaholics ski marathon, Robin won the eleven-mile race two years in a row.

Jersey Ski-Ters Water Ski Club Honors George Blair

> September 17, 1980
>
> Dear Fellow Ski-Ters:
>
> At our meeting last month, when you presented me with a plaque of honorary membership, and a beautifully decorated celebration cake, it was absolutely the biggest surprise of my life.
>
> When our president, Ted Reiss, said all those nice things about me, recounting my long membership in the club, my perpetual participation in our ski shows, how my wife and four daughters also have been involved as show performers or officers, and the marks I have made in competitions—it was the first time in my life I became totally speechless.

Therefore, I want to take this means of expressing to you my deepest gratitude for your thoughtfulness. That night will be one of my most treasured memories.

As I look back over the past twenty-five years, it is easy to see that waterskiing, barefooting, kite flying, hydrofoiling, and club activities have played a very large role in my life. And if God is willing, I might turn out to be one of the most active honorary members that this club has ever had.

I am sorry that I will not be attending the meeting on September 19, as I am planning to be at the second World Barefoot Championships in San Francisco.

Again, many many thanks!

Sincerely yours,
George Blair

Chapter 6

Blair Family Rhythm

George and Dorothy continued to juggle the multiple businesses and activities each was involved with. The baby picture service continued to grow, expanding to hospitals all over the United States. To reflect the superior quality of his business compared to his competitors, George changed the name to Hospital Portrait Service (HPS). George expanded to a new service that would provide copies of x-rays and office records on microfilm to minimize storage space, which he called The Microfilm Center.

Dorothy and George enjoyed making time for social activities. "Dad and Mom were beautiful dancers. Whenever they were on the dance floor, people would clear the floor to watch them. They danced ballroom and Latin dances. At home, when the spirit was right, we pushed the furniture in the living room to the side to make more room for dancing. They taught us the waltz and fox trot, the merengue, cha-cha, and limbo. We danced up a frenzy, and sometimes we had to open the front door for fresh cool air when we got too hot," Robin remembered.

On Wednesdays, George played the drums in a jazz combo in Tinton Falls. There was always music in the house. He often practiced with his musician friends in the basement on his yellow drum set. (Yellow was becoming his signature color, as will be explained later in Chapter 10.) It was a good way for him to release some of his indefatigable energy.

Dad had a brown faux fur, full-length coat, from his college days, that hung in the hall closet," Robin said. "We called it the Bear Coat.

Once in a while, Dad would take the coat out and throw it over himself, get down on all fours, and make big roaring sounds at us. Of course, we knew he was under the coat, but he made a convincing scary bear."

"Talking about getting scared," Robin continued, "when it was time for us to go upstairs to bed, he would sneak up behind us and pound the bottom step as if he were bounding up after us. For many years after, we always scurried up the stairs, thinking of Dad chasing after us!"

"We had a fireplace in our living room. In the basement; a little trap door was the clean-out for the ashes. Dad would tell us, 'Never open that little trap door because that is where I keep my Superman suit. I never know when I will need it!' To us, he was a hero, so it was easy to believe."

Besides being our hero, George was also a statistician. He even recorded mundane things, such as the monthly weight of each family member on a graph. The daughters were not given their allowances until their weight was entered on the chart.

The expense and planning for children's birthday parties could be overwhelming, especially with four girls in the family. George's solution was to allow each girl to have a party every five years, at five, ten, and fifteen years old. That infrequency might sound a little strict, but the girls really looked forward to those special parties, if they were for one of them or their sisters. Dorothy, an artistic, creative mom, planned themed parties such as ballerina, treasure hunts, and the Wild West. They were always at the Blairs' Buttonwood home. Everyone helped decorate and participate in the planning. Nothing was outsourced.

Donna recalls, "We didn't have air conditioning in the house in the 1950s. Dad had a sprinkler hose installed on the ridge of the slate roof. In theory, if the roof were cooler, the house would also be cooler. When the water was on, it looked like it was raining! He also installed an attic fan that would draw hot air out of the house. Eventually, we had window air conditioner units."

"Dad played as hard as he worked," GeeGee remembers. "If he came home from the office at lunchtime, he would take a ten-minute power nap. I think it might have been a holdover from the years recuperating from back surgery. The coins from his pockets would fall out when he lay down. After he went back to the office, we quickly searched in the cushions for coins."

Being fastidious, George hated the bathroom soap getting slimy on the bottom from sitting in a puddle of water. He discovered a clever way of keeping the soap dry by using a small metal disk that was pressed into the soap. A compatible soap holder was attached to the wall above the sink. The soap holder extended a few inches from the wall and had a magnet. The metal disk in the soap held firmly to the magnet holder, keeping it high and dry.

A house rule was that the telephone should be answered on the first ring, but by the third at the very latest. A pad and pen had to be next to each phone and a message written if appropriate. Because the two businesses had started in the home, a phone was in every room except the bathrooms. This was in the days before cordless phones. Three lines ran into the house, and a Hold button was on each phone. The girls learned early on how to be competent when answering a business call.

Later, those notepads were embellished. Imagine a 3" x 4" memo pad with a portrait the size of a postage stamp of George in the corner. It reminded the family that messages are an important means of communication. When someone received one of these memos from him, there he was staring at her or him from his photo.

A management concept that George carried into family life was the rooming arrangement. The Buttonwood house had three bedrooms. The four daughters were assigned to rooms so that the older ones could help the younger ones. Donna (first born) roomed with Carrie (third), GeeGee (second) roomed with Robin (fourth). At the rectangular dinner table, the six seats were grouped so that Donna and Carrie were on one side, GeeGee and Robin on the other. George and Dorothy were at the head seats at each end, GeeGee and Carrie at their father's end, Donna and Robin at their mother's end. In the center of the table was an elegant turntable (lazy susan) that contained salt and pepper, vinegar and oil, jam or jelly, butter, etc. This made access to these items available to everyone, a more efficient method than "Please pass the…."

There was also a rotation for setting the table and washing dishes. Each daughter had designated days of the week. Dishwashing was facilitated by a handheld gadget that George had installed on the kitchen faucet through which the water flowed. On the end of the device was a brush, and at the push of a button, detergent was dispensed with the water. The brush helped scour the dishes.

In keeping with George's interest in ingenious devices and healthful living, he had a central vacuum installed in the house. It was quite unusual and innovative in the 1950s to have a built-in vacuum system. Because it was vented outside, no dust or allergens were recirculated in the interior air. Another benefit was that there was nothing heavy to carry as in traditional portable models, and the motor was powerful.

With four daughters to manage, George had a plan for date night. "The young men who came to pick us up had to be scrutinized by dad," Robin recalled. "He was positioned in his chair in the living room. Our date was ushered in to face Mr. Blair, who asked sternly where they were going and what time they would return. He made the boys' knees buckle a little and put the fear of God in them. Consequently, we were rarely home late, unless we knew our parents were out also."

"He also had a one-way mirror installed in the front door so he could look out, but people on the other side could not look in. You never knew whether he was watching you. So much for good-night kisses," GeeGee said.

Robin recalls, "For some years when we were children, our family drove from New Jersey to Florida. The drive south was always an adventure. It was before the days of DVD players, cell phones, and iPads with games. Instead, we played the 1950s car games of identifying license plates, or "I spy with my little eye something that is _____ (name a color)," and singing songs. Since our mother had a beautiful voice and was an avid Girl Scout, she knew all sorts of fun songs, some with rounds. Dad would always join in. It broke the monotony of the long drive. He did almost all of the driving. We would also stop at roadside attractions such as the 'upside down house.' Historical markers were another good excuse to take a break. Mom taught us several dinnertime graces that we sang in harmony, such as 'Alleluia Chorus,' 'The Wayfarers Grace,' and 'Dona Nobis Pacem.' One of our family traditions carries on today. The Blair daughters sing grace before holiday dinner festivities. When George said grace, his favorite, which he would say with gravitas, was: 'For friends and for family, for faith and for food, we give thanks to God the gracious giver of all great gifts. Amen.'"

Always fond of gadgets, George had a device to alert him if he was getting sleepy while driving. It fit in his ear, and if his chin dropped down, it would sound an alarm. He often chewed gum as a distraction and would have a selection of gum lined up on his dashboard as a treat for the girls. There would be Beemans, Black Jack, Teaberry, and Clove, but never bubble gum. The gum had to be disposed of properly wrapped in paper.

When the family stayed for several winter months, the girls were enrolled in Pinecrest Day School in Fort Lauderdale, Florida. On one such car trip on a quiet strip of road in Georgia, late at night, George decided to coast down the long hilly road. By the time he got to the bottom, he was going really fast. He loved to coast to save on gas, probably a technique he used back in the college and Depression days. However, as the car started climbing up the next big hill, the family heard a police siren. The Blairs' car was the only one on the road at that point, so George slowed to a stop. A state trooper walked up to his window and asked for ID, which he promptly gave him, but George also asked, "What seems to be the problem officer?"

The trooper replied, "Well, sir, I clocked you speeding. You were going twenty-five miles per hour over the speed limit." George said, "Oh, I can explain. I was just showing my daughters how you can save money on gas by coasting down the hill—let gravity do the work!" The girls can't recall what else was said because they were too scared that something bad would happen, but George and the officer seemed to part ways on good terms. George got a warning—no ticket.

"Same time the next year," Robin recalls, "as we are driving through Georgia in the Caddy, stuffed to the gills with luggage for six people and a black standard poodle, Cyrano de Bergerac, we came to the same spot where there was a series of hills. Dad again put the car in neutral and coasted down the hill. It was déjà vu! While climbing up the next hill, we heard a police siren. Dad knew it was for him so he pulled over. A state trooper walked up to the car and asked for ID. He looked at Dad's driver's license and then said to Dad, 'You're the fella I stopped last year on your way to Florida.' They started to chat, and when the officer looked into the car, he said, 'Let's not meet again next year.' I think we flew to Florida most of the time after that!"

"Dad was usually in a hurry," GeeGee remembers, "because he always had more to accomplish than time would allow. Often, if he were dropping us off at high school on his way to his office or taking us to lessons (ballet, baton twirling, horse riding, piano), he would slow the car and tell us to get ready. We were expected to jump out of the car when it was barely moving so he never had to come to a full stop."

Robin recalls, "Dad had an uncanny sense about him. When he wanted you for any reason or wanted to know where you were, he would find you (before GPS). As an employee of HPS, I had the privilege of driving a company car, maybe the blue Buick, the green wagon, or my favorite, the red Thunderbird with a black vinyl top.

"I had a new boyfriend and was being evasive about my plans. We were tooling up the Garden State Parkway on the way to New York City. I stopped to pay the toll (before the days of EZ pass). The toll collector looked at me and asked, 'Is your name Robin Blair?' Absolutely astonished at his question, I replied, 'Yes.' 'Then you need to call your father immediately,' he said. How did Dad do that?

George also liked to live spontaneously. He expected you to be ready to go within fifteen minutes even if it might be for an overnight trip. He often would toss something to you and yell, "Think fast," giving you barely time to react, always honing your reflexes. He loved a challenge. He was a harsh critic who would scold, scream, and make faces when you did not measure up. But he was equally exuberant when things went well. He was very expressive, laughing, clapping you on the back, shaking your hand, and making you feel like a hero. He just never held back and he was the life of the party.

His four daughters grew up decisive, sharp-witted, and independent just when the mid-twentieth century women's liberation movement was at its fullest expression. Today, they are athletic, fit, and adaptable. They saw their father change his hair and beard style and wear trendy new fashions all his life, so they keep up with the changing times as well.

George and Dorothy's oldest daughter, Donna, married Charles Matches in 1959. In October 1962, Donna gave birth to the Blairs' first grandchild, Robert Charles, known as Robbie. The Blairs were thrilled to welcome a boy into the family. When Donna and Charles' marriage ended, George became a "father figure" to little Robbie. He took Robbie out on the water with him and taught him to water ski.

Now a single mother, Donna was on her Lambretta motor scooter when, at a red light, a handsome man pulled up on his motorcycle. He promptly asked her for a date. Bernie Yaged loved water and was an accomplished swimmer. It didn't take long before he became best buddies with George. When Bernie asked for Donna's hand in marriage, George was thrilled. Bernie became a very good skier and an instructor at the ski school. He and George also shared a love of music and often jammed together after ski sessions with Bernie playing the piano.

"George taught me to barefoot ski, and we did a lot of ski racing," Bernie recalled. "We skied for twenty-five miles down the river. I don't think George and I ever lost—sometimes we did two races in a day. We did that for four years—we were very competitive! George would do everything at 100 percent. Whatever he did, he did it with a positive attitude."

George and Bernie often raced in very rough water and in extreme conditions—such as 32° on New Year's Day. Bernie recalled:

> Some of the best moments between us was when we would win a race. It's a huge effort between skier and driver. During one race, I tried to tell George to slow down in rough water; I thought I would fall. He nodded his head and laughed. I continued going through two-foot waves, shaking my head at him. It was then I realized, we think we have limits—we say, "I can't. I can't"—but someone else shows us we have no limits. That's what George taught me.

A similar testimony is from Garry Barton, barefoot champion, who said, "George taught me to never give up, even when the water was rough. 'Go out there and Do It,' he instructed."

Bernie and Donna parted in 1974, but Bernie continued to be part of the family and considered George one of his best friends. Their twenty-seven-year age difference simply didn't matter.

Chuck Sidun, Bernie, and George were often a trio. Chuck was almost forty years younger than George. Chuck said he and George were not aware of the age differences; they were just barefooting buddies. "George was a mentor to me in business. He grew up during the Depression, and he had business principles related to that experience. He truly enjoyed working and enjoyed the benefits of his hard work. George's joy in life was apparent to everyone," said Chuck. "He loved an audience, and he loved to show off. His favorite part of show skiing was hearing the crowd cheer. After too many painful backward barefoot falls, George vowed to invent a brace that would protect skiers' necks from whiplash."

"I remember him being persnickety about his boat and boathouse," Chuck added. George took great pride in his immaculate boathouse, which was a splash of yellow inside and out. George always drove sleek yellow boats, provided others with—guess what?—yellow skis, wake boards, inner tubes, ski vests, and even monogrammed yellow towels for après ski. There was a yellow guestbook for people to sign when they entered the boat house. He liked to keep track of everything in his life.

George loved boats from the time he built an ice boat in his attic as a child to sailing boats on Lake Erie, to working on a sidewheel ferry boat where he first saw Dorothy, to racing in the Hudson River Powerboat Marathon, to ice boating, to having the fastest water ski boat on the river. His powerful ski boats threw small wakes and had customized gold anodized instruments and telescoping ski booms. He was always searching for the best boat, owning a variety from Hydrodyne, Donzi, Ski Nautique, Ski Extreme, Correct Craft, MasterCraft, Malibu, and finally a Sanger Boat.

George Alfred Blair, born 1915

Blair boys, George, Bobby, Laurel

Blair Family 1953: Donna, Robin, George, Dorothy, GeeGee, Carrie

George & Dorothy Blair and his sister's family at Christmas dinner 1966

Don't Wait for Life to Happen—Make it Happen 49

Blair family water skiing, Christmas card 1958

Blair family ice boating, Christmas card 1963

George Blair businesses, 1961

George with his third grandson, Theodore.
Note the IBM computer terminal, 1982

George with his standard poodle, ChaCha
Photo credit: Monroe Edelstein

George and his alter ego, Mercury

Section II
Fame and Change

1973–1985

"Live your life like you like it!"

— "Banana" George Blair

Chapter 7
Changing Course

Unknown to Dorothy, George was making time to see one of his water ski students. He had fallen in love with her and had to make a choice.

Dorothy was devastated when George told her he wanted to end their marriage. At first, she tried everything she could to save their marriage, but it soon became apparent that George had made up his mind. He was spending more time away from home. After a separation from Dorothy, he filed for divorce.

In September 1973, George married JoAnne White in the private home of close friends in Edison, New Jersey. They settled down in Red Bank, just a few blocks from the HPS office. Their penthouse apartment overlooked the Navesink River, and the yellow ski boat was docked a few steps away from the building's riverfront entrance.

George was happy to begin every day—around 6 a.m.—barefooting for about a mile down the river. JoAnne usually drove for him, but then Robbie, the oldest grandson, started working part-time for Fogging Unlimited, and he took over the morning driving and skiing on the days he worked.

Later, the penthouse and its terrace became the gathering place for family birthdays and to watch the Red Bank fireworks for the Fourth of July. The long hallway in the apartment became a drag strip for the small electric toy cars the grandsons got for Christmas.

JoAnne's background included both television programming and publishing. She worked for NET, the forerunner of National Educational Television, NBC, and the *International Herald Tribune* in Paris.

One night at the penthouse, when she switched the TV on to NBC, a new program was announced. "This is *The Prime of Your Life*" was the catchy song announcing the format: a program for active middle-aged people.

JoAnne thought to herself: "This looks as though it would be a perfect show for George—I wonder whether I know anyone connected with it." She watched the credit lines and, sure enough, Milton Wyatt, someone she had worked with, was film director. JoAnne telephoned him.

"Milt, George would be perfect for *The Prime of Your Life*!" Milt had not yet met George, but he knew JoAnne well and trusted her judgment. A few weeks later, Joe Michaels, host of the show along with Arlene Francis, arrived with a film crew.

The crew was warmly greeted by JoAnne and George as well as friend Chuck Sidun, who had agreed to drive the boat for the shooting, and Robbie who was scheduled to appear with his grandfather.

When the shooting was over, everyone gathered around the dining room table where a beautiful big cake was the centerpiece. "Welcome Prime of Your Life" was written in yellow frosting on its top.

The show received good reviews and was Banana George's first national TV appearance. (More about the name Banana George in Chapter 9.) As you know, it was followed by many others.

Transitions

For George's daughters, the end of their parents' marriage was difficult. Their family life had been exciting, compelling, and filled with incredible experiences. How could this seemingly perfect marriage be over? The daughters loved both parents. Donna and her son Robbie lived nearby in New Jersey. Robin was living in New York City working at an art gallery and studying. Carrie was teaching horse riding and competing while living in Florida and Virginia. GeeGee, who had moved back to Buttonwood after living and studying in India for a year, saw firsthand the pain her mother felt during this time.

The four daughters took some time to adjust to this new arrangement. But JoAnne was a loving person, always welcoming them to the penthouse. Over the years, she hosted celebrations and holiday parties for the girls and their families in Red Bank, and then later in Florida and, of course, New York City. She was also generous in loaning them the apartment in Paris that George bought for her.

In the meantime, Dorothy showed her resilience. Her faith, social connections, and volunteer activities were a strong foundation that helped her through the difficult time. Several years after the divorce, she married Robert I. Manson, her ardent admirer, and the international vice-president for C. R. Bard, a leading medical technology manufacturer. She and Bob traveled extensively around the world. They lived in the same Tudor brick home on Buttonwood that George and Dorothy had purchased in 1946 until Dorothy's sudden death October 17, 1995.

Dorothy knew the importance of volunteering one's time and talents. She was active in many civic, charitable, and artistic organizations. After many years serving on the Borough Council, she was elected Mayor of Shrewsbury and served three terms. She was the first woman to hold the office. A sixteen-acre park at the Shrewsbury Borough Hall was named for her. Dorothy also remained involved with the Monmouth Council of Girl Scouts, was named Woman of the Year by Zonta, and again by the Jay-Cees. She was the first woman deacon of her church, and she was honored as Headliner of the Year 1988 by her alma mater, Wayne State University.

GeeGee married Al Turrisi in 1974 in an early morning Hindu fire ceremony in Shrewsbury, performed by Swami Atmananda. The wedding was the first time since their divorce that Dorothy and George were together at a family event, and they made a point of being courteous toward one another. In July 1975, GeeGee gave birth to George's second grandson, Marcus. Meanwhile, George, always on the lookout for a loyal employee, enlisted Al to work first with Donna at Fogging Unlimited and then as sales manager for HPS.

Fogging Unlimited Changes Hands

HPS required George's focus as it expanded nationwide. In 1973, Fogging Unlimited lost its general manager and the business was faltering. Donna was standing in the office one day while George was expressing his frustration with the situation.

"Why don't you just identify the problem and fix it—or sell the business?" Donna suggested.

"Why don't *you* find out what's wrong?" he challenged her.

"Okay. I'll work for six months and see whether I can find the problem."

"I had no business experience—I had just graduated with a teaching degree," Donna recalled. "I had no background in bugs—except what I heard around the dinner table."

Being the boss' daughter, and a woman in a male-dominated business, was not easy for Donna. George taught her the basics, and then she was on her own. She learned everything she could about the business—going out on every call and studying the service model, which was not as efficient as it could have been.

"I dove into it 100 percent from the start," Donna said. "I was involved with the New Jersey Pest Control Association and I wrote its newsletter for years. I was the first female vice president of NJPCA, and the first female on the National Pest Control Association. I guess my father taught me, "If you do something, be fully involved—'Do It' to the best of your ability." Donna successfully operated the business for the next eighteen years.

Swami Atmananda came to the Blair house in 1970 when he accompanied GeeGee on her return from India. He was a young Hindu swami with thick black hair and traditional orange robes. This was his first experience traveling outside his country. His main activity before meeting George Blair had been studying Sanskrit scriptures, chanting, and meditation.

At the Blair household, he was immediately thrown into a whirlwind of activity. It was winter and George was giving rides on the sled hooked behind his Cadillac on the snow-packed road around Buttonwood. Swamiji joined George's grandson Robbie, then seven years old, on the sled. This helped Swamiji overcome his fear of the risky-looking endeavor. It was exhilarating. Next they went ice boating and snow skiing.

Swamiji learned that George was adept at awakening the inner child in people. "When we grow up, we often forget how to have fun and miss out on enjoying life. George knew how to bring out the youthful spirit in people. I wanted to encounter God in my spiritual practice, but he made me realize that divinity can also be experienced in the outside world."

Becoming a Banker

At a Kiwanis Club talk George gave in 1996 in Red Bank, he said, "My banking story starts in 1946 when I had a dream. The dream was to bring joy to new mothers and fathers by taking pictures of their newborn babies in the hospital.

"I naively went to the Fidelity Bank on Broad Street, Red Bank, and told them of my dream and how I needed to borrow capital for my start-up. They laughed me right out the front door.

"After picking myself up, I tried the same at the Merchants Bank also on Broad Street. Well, it took Mr. McQueen only a couple of minutes to say no. In this case, though, it was a kinder no and without any laughs. He even gave me a couple of minutes of sympathy and advice.

"I promptly gave Mr. McQueen the privilege of mortgaging my home for my start-up cash.

"Years later, in the 1970s, an enterprising young lawyer, Steve Ingram, who had been working for the New Jersey State Banking Commission, approached me about starting a hometown bank. His invitation fell on very receptive ears for two reasons: First, because my father, my uncle, and my grandfather had all been bankers, it was already in my blood. Secondly, I wanted to be connected with a small bank that would not laugh at budding entrepreneurs.

"The Shrewsbury State Bank opened its doors on Broad Street in Shrewsbury in 1974. The enthusiastic acceptance of our hometown bank warmed my heart, a dream come true. The bank was successful right from the start. My skills in administration and finance as well as my business standing in the community were especially valuable and Steve recognized that."

Although George was twenty-seven years older than Steve, they were, as Steve's wife Terry recalled, "joined at the hip." Steve served as George's personal attorney. As founders of the bank, they served on the

Board of Directors and had the oversight of several departments. They worked on marketing together, but George was most proud of "his" audit department. The bank was Triple-A rated.

In 2004, the Shrewsbury State Bank was sold to a larger bank, the Valley National Bank. George was very instrumental in the negotiations for the sale. He was even featured on a billboard for the bank, barefoot skiing, that encouraged kids to start a savings account.

After George's death, Gerry Lipkin, president of Valley National Bank, wrote to the family:

> I was deeply saddened today when I learned of George's passing. He had such a wonderful zest for life and a spirit that totally belied his age.
>
> His love for waterskiing kept him young as well as an inspiration to all who knew him. His passion for the color yellow enabled him to stand out in a crowd.
>
> Unfortunately, our paths did not cross until his ninetieth year. I'm sure that his feisty attitude would have made him a person I certainly would have enjoyed spending time with on numerous occasions. His business acumen was respected and appreciated by his fellow board members at Shrewsbury State Bank.

Chapter 8
Relentless Tenacity

"I DIDN'T KNOW the meaning of the word 'tenacious' until later in life when I realized, 'That's my dad—he never gives up,'" Robin said. "He stuck it out—like walking into a prospective hospital multiple times to pitch his business. He would follow up his visits with a thank you note and phone calls. He learned everyone's name, overwhelming people with his charm. This tenacity usually paid off.

"When Dad was making the transition from skis to barefoot starts," Robin continues, "especially deep-water starts, it was really difficult for him to get the hang of it. I was on spring break from school and went to Florida to be with him. I witnessed the relentless wipeouts time after time on the first day. The instructor was good. The boat driver was good. What was wrong? On the second day of this punishment, he finally aced it! Eureka! What jubilation! The instructor had never experienced a spirit like my dad's."

In his diary, George wrote, "It is the mark of a developed mind to be able to stick to a difficulty that one is attempting to master." (Quoted from the 1913 book, *Human Behavior: A First Book of Psychology for Teachers* by Stephen Sheldon Colvin, William Chandler Bagley.) That "sticktoitiveness" was so much a part of George that it penetrated every aspect of his life.

When Frank Fetter was eight years old, he took water ski lessons from George, and later, he learned to barefoot. His family ended up buying George's boat. George taught Frank a valuable lesson about tenacity: Face adversity in life, but don't allow it to become a defining factor—don't accept defeat or failure.

"One day, we were out on the water and our motor wouldn't start," Frank recalled. "George was giving a lesson and saw that we were in trouble. He came over and tried starting the motor—it wouldn't start, so he checked all the obvious things. He pulled and pulled at the motor until he was exhausted. He did everything in life that way—he just wouldn't quit. Finally, he towed our boat in behind his."

Frank once asked George his process for making business decisions. "You have to be very honest with your assessment of every decision. Figure out what you will get back, compare the risks and benefits, and then the answer will be as plain as the nose on your face," said George.

While he was in college, Frank worked for George at the ski school. He had another interest: George's youngest daughter Robin. The two got married and had two boys: Theodore (Ted/Theo) born in August 1982 and Oliver born in October 1986.

Grandfather

Four grandsons, wow! George flourished in his role as grandfather, modeling a well-rounded, vital, caring person. He loved challenging his grandsons and being challenged by them. His grandsons called him "GB," his initials. The label "grandfather" did not seem fitting.

On school holidays, George sometimes invited all the grandsons for a boys-only vacation in Colorado or Florida to snow board or water ski and barefoot with him. After skiing, they played music together, or *Space Invaders*, ping pong, pool, or jumped in the hot tub.

George supplied yellow snowboards, and yellow boarding suits with matching helmets for each of them—the whole works! It was impressive and eye-catching to see the Banana Team doing tricks, jumps, and boarding down the mountain as a group. Their nights were spent making healthy dinners, regaling each other with stories, and playing games.

It's Not Over Until I Win

George wrote in 1994:

> In my Winter Haven, Florida home one mile from Cypress Gardens, I have one of the original video games—*Space Invaders*. It must be more than twenty years old and I have racked up thousands of games without one operational flaw.

The thick glass top itself must weigh thirty-five pounds and the whole table-style console over 200 pounds. Compare this to a Nintendo that weighs maybe eight ounces! In all the years I have owned it, I must have played over 5,000 games.

Whenever any of my four grandsons come to visit, they enjoy trying to beat me. One night last year, my twelve-year-old grandson was playing against me, and as the clock ticked on, I finally said, "It's about time for bed, Teddy." He answered, "No, not yet. It's not over until I win." So, the game resumed and Ted finally beat me and he said, "Now we can go to bed."

The message was loud and clear. There are no excuses for ever giving up because it's not over until you win. A man can succeed at anything he has a passion for as long as he has confidence and faith.

Water Skiing Stories

George created an annual endurance barefoot water ski tournament and dubbed it the Blairfoot Bananza. It took a great deal of effort to organize this event, but George got a lot of help. Every year, it was a real test for George to see how far and long he could remain upright on the water. But here's the thing: He wasn't just competing with teens, young adults, and men half his age—he was always competing against himself and pushing himself to improve each run. As a result, age became meaningless. In fact, at the age of eighty-three and eight months, George came in second for the longest endurance time (3:45) in a pool of competitors of all age groups.

"I'm proud of the fact that even though I'm in the senior division, I was able to come up with the second best time out of all the sixty-five competing," said George in an article published in the *Florida News Chief*.

Because he was often the oldest competitive barefoot water skier in his division, George was constantly setting records. At the 1999 Orlando Tournament, George slalomed a 4.7, more than double the average score of intermediate skiers half his age.

George may very well be the oldest person to barefoot water ski backwards. In the late 1980s, George met John Clemmons and John's uncle, Mike Murphy. They often skied on the Colorado River on the border of California close to Arizona. Mike was known for his expertise on the hydrofoil skis and hydrofoil chair. He demonstrated flips and helicopters over the wake, and he taught George how to ride with a beautiful girl on his shoulders. One afternoon, a group of eight skiers (George included) set an informal world record for the most hydrofoil skiers behind one boat.

When it came to learning how to barefoot backwards, George expressed his frustration to John about his difficulties in getting up backwards. John had just learned a new technique from Chris Harris—a five-time European Barefoot Champion.

"Let me show you this new technique," John told George. George tried the new technique, and on the second day, he was skiing backwards. John snapped a picture of George with a happy smile on his face and seaweed hanging down from the handle.

Necessity is the mother of invention. George identified two problems that he encountered with barefooting: uncomfortable groin cups that kept slipping down and a very sore neck after falling backwards. George went to work finding a new, contoured cup that stayed in place during barefooting maneuvers. He joined forces with a designer, and they called it—what else?—the Banana Cup. He trademarked the design and eventually sold it to Bike Corporation. It's the same contour that you see in today's men's athletic cups. See photo page 95.

To protect his neck from the brutal backward skiing falls, George invented a "Banana Boa." It was a waterproof neck brace that prevented whiplash and saved many a skier from an injured neck after falling backwards. George applied for a patent, and it was officially designated a Skier's Safety Harness. The patent description was: "A pair of back straps, a pair of neck straps and a linking web combine to hold a neck cushion in place for protecting the neck of an athlete."

George continued to ski with John and Mike and several others on the river. "Can I borrow your car?" George asked John one afternoon. He was gone for about two hours.

"You know that house on the hill?" George said when he returned.

"Yeah, Mr. K's place?"

"No, it's not; I just bought that house." George grinned.

The house became George's "Man Cave," and it was the site of many conversations and cookouts. "We taught him about barefooting, and George taught us about life," John said. "He told me, 'You can't buy time or buy your youth again. You can always make money, but you can't make time.' That's why he lived each day to the fullest—he knew he wouldn't be here forever. He was the last to pass out at night and the first to get up in the morning."

Chapter 9
Becoming Banana George

WHEN GEORGE RAN The Family Ski School at the second location at Mirror Lake in Edison, New Jersey, it was next to a private swim club. It was there he met a talented artist, Bobbi Goodman. Her whole family learned to water ski with George and they got such a kick out of him. She gave him a gift that would set his brand in visible motion.

"People had been calling me 'The Banana Man' or 'Banana George' for quite a while because I would always bring a bunch of bananas for my pupils and their families," George said. "One day, Bobbi presented me with a shirt that had a banana and *George* hand-painted on it. I wore that shirt a lot from then on and still have it, more than fifty years later. It was then that the name Banana George really stuck."

Everywhere he went, George handed out his postcard-size photo business card with his statistics, and gave out bananas. You couldn't walk through the airport with him without having to stop every couple of steps. He would hand out the cards and bananas and engage in conversation. He was a standout in his all yellow, Colonel Sanders-looking suit and ten-gallon hat. So many people recognized him from the commercials (Armor All, Cheerios, etc.) and Cypress Gardens shows. He was buying boxes of Chiquita bananas, and soon, photos of George and bananas were showing up everywhere.

Cy Cyr, who took the photograph on this book's cover, recalled meeting George on a few occasions and remembered his passion for bananas:

I first met Banana George when I was twelve, on summer vacation in Florida. I guess that was 1989. I still have the autograph he signed for me. It was a true thrill to photograph him in 2005 for *Waterski Magazine*. At that time, I asked Mr. Blair how many bananas he'd eaten in his life, and I think he said, "One hundred thousand." I didn't know whether he was kidding with me or not, but with a name like 'Banana,' I took it as fact.

In December 1992, George and JoAnne were sitting in the kitchen of their Florida home when the phone rang.

George answered and listened intently as the caller presented an offer for George. Would he be interested in representing Chiquita Bananas on a media tour?

"Do you know how long I've been waiting for this call?" George replied. He had been giving out Chiquita bananas for years without the company's sponsorship, but now it would be supporting his efforts at a whole new level.

George and the Chiquita company crafted a relationship to promote bananas—an estimated two tons per year. For every tournament and media appearance, Chiquita shipped out cases of bananas. "Each week, when we were home in Florida, a big truck would pull up in our driveway and a delivery man would emerge with at least one forty-pound case of Chiquita bananas to leave at our back entrance," JoAnne recalled. "George was doing many overseas exhibitions at that time and Chiquita started following us around the world. When we notified the company, a delivery of bananas would arrive at our hotel in France, Germany, Austria—wherever George was skiing."

Despite keeping the bananas in the all-yellow garage or the all-yellow laundry room, the smell permeated the house. One afternoon, JoAnne went to a hair salon for her usual shampoo and cut. As she relaxed in the chair, a familiar scent wafted in the air. For a minute, JoAnne thought she was imagining things.

"Do I smell bananas?"

The shampoo girl gave her a big smile. "Oh, yes; this is our new banana rinse!"

Wanderlust

George and JoAnne headed down to Baton Rouge, Louisiana, where her mother, Irene, was living, for a combined family and business trip. Irene was delighted to see them, and they spent the first evening catching up over dinner.

The next morning, George and JoAnne took off in two different directions. It was pouring rain. JoAnne had HPS appointments with hospitals in and around Monroe. Meanwhile, George managed to visit hospitals in Dallas before he was caught in a sandstorm.

When he finally came to the end of the sandstorm, he thought he was seeing a mirage: signs for a barefoot water ski tournament!

That night he called JoAnne in Baton Rouge. "You won't believe this, but I went to a barefoot tournament in Tyler, Texas today!" George bubbled over with excitement. "I was watching the tournament when this guy named William Farrell—he's the tournament director—asked why I wasn't entered. I said, 'I can't start competing at my age.' And he said, 'Why not?' He said they'd let me ski at the end of the tournament! This is the perfect place for someone like me. I'll call you later, I'm off to the site."

There wasn't much conversation about the hospital business as George was about to head back to the tournament site. Before hanging up, he told JoAnne he was staying another night.

"I have to go now; I'm going out with some of the guys. I'll call you again tomorrow. Ski ya later," he said.

George entered the slalom and start events. To his surprise, he ended up with a third-place medal in slalom. "The guy I tied with was about twenty-two-years-old, and in the run-off, I beat him," George said in a *Water Skier* magazine interview. "He was mortified to be beaten by a sixty-three-year-old intruder. Afterward, we all went out together and had pizza, and I became well-acquainted with all these people I'd been hearing about. I was in Seventh Heaven."

George was giddy with a newfound passion for barefooting competition. It took his skills to a whole new level. Even though he had been barefooting for seventeen years and performing in ski shows, he was a beginner in competition. To compete in tournaments, George had to learn new tricks on the water and complete as many of those tricks as he could in twenty (later it became fifteen) seconds. At sixty-three-years old, George was at an age where it was practically unheard of to compete in an extreme sport.

"George watched and learned; he met everyone at the tournament and was thrilled with the camaraderie," said the tournament director. "He was inspired and tournaments became his passion. As he became older, we created new divisions for him. He called other competitors, 'Banana Chasers,' for everyone was chasing him."

The following summer, George called John Cornish, the director of the Eastern Region. "Do you have a division for me?" he asked.

"If you show up and ski, I'll create a division for you," John said. It was just the second year of the Eastern Region barefoot tournaments. Everything was in its infancy in the sport.

George showed up in a camper and parked at the edge of the lake. The skiers were amazed at George's high energy and enthusiasm despite being an "old man" in a sport that caters to the younger crowd. This was just the beginning of George's involvement with the American Barefoot Club. He was subsequently the first person to be named "Man of the Year" by the club due to his guidance and generosity.

At the Nationals that year, George met a young, up-and-coming barefooter named Ron Scarpa. Ron was just fifteen years old and skiing his first national tournament. He took one look at George, dressed in yellow from head to toe (complete with see-through clogs filled with yellow goldfish), and was instantly intrigued. "I fell in love with the guy," Ron recalled. "Not a lot of teenagers fall in love with old people, you know, but he was such a cool guy." Even Ron's high school friends enjoyed hanging around George despite the huge age gap.

When Ron arrived home after the tournament, he sat down to write George a letter. He was not one to write letters, but he was so moved by this extraordinary barefooter that he wanted to reach out to him.

Ron and George continued their friendship at every tournament. Ron opened his own ski school in Florida and went on to become a five-time World Barefoot Champion. The two of them skied together whenever George vacationed in Florida. In the boat, between sets, Ron peppered George with questions on how to run his ski business. George listened intently, but he responded with a question about improving his tumble-turn technique. "I'm not going to answer your barefooting question until you answer my business question," Ron said, laughing.

Ron did his best to keep George safe on the water, but as a friend instead of an instructor, it wasn't easy reining him in. George wanted to push everything to the limit. "He was reckless and a risk-taker, and I was just a kid," Ron said. After a couple of falls, George was always pushing for one more try, one more run, but Ron learned to hold firm to keep him in one piece.

One day, on the way to a tournament in Florida, Ron spotted George's yellow Cadillac on the side of Highway 4. He pulled over quickly and ran to the car.

"You need help?"

George was rummaging through the trunk, double-checking to see whether he had brought all of his barefooting gear for the tournament. "No, I'm good. Thanks! Ski ya later."

Ron got back on the highway and was going faster than usual, trying to make up for lost time. Five minutes later, the yellow Caddy zipped right by going 90 to 100 mph.

"It was like I was standing still; he blew right past me," Ron recalled. "Here I was thinking an old man needed help on the side of the road—then he goes past me like *I'm* the old man!"

As Ron learned, George was not a man of patience. When he wanted something done, it had to be done…yesterday. "George was always in a hurry," Al Turrisi recalled. "Whenever he had to go through a toll booth, he didn't want to waste time, so he lined his quarters up in a trigger-pull coin dispenser. He would roll through the tollbooth and shoot the quarter out of the window—right into the toll basket—without stopping."

Chapter 10
Yellow Fever

People always asked George, "Why yellow?" In response, George would joke, "I have one story and it's patented! Yellow is so dominant; the other colors just don't turn me on, and I think it really reflects my sunny attitude."

Slowly but surely, yellow took over George's persona. JoAnne didn't have much choice but to embrace the various shades of yellow in their lives. It started innocently enough: George ordered a custom yellow wetsuit. By the end of his career, he had amassed closets full of all-yellow wetsuits, a yellow custom-made tuxedo, yellow shirts (many with banana designs), yellow ties, yellow suits and jackets, yellow snake-skin cowboy boots, yellow lizard dress shoes, yellow 10-gallon hats, yellow T-shirts, and rarely-worn yellow underwear. George liked to hang free; jockey and boxer shorts were not found in his wardrobe. He did, however, for protection, wear a yellow bikini and yellow Banana Cup, of his own design under his barefoot wetsuit.

George said all that yellow made it easy to pick out what he was going to wear that day! Guests looking at the array of yellow in the closets were amazed. It just happened to be a coincidence that George's favorite fruit was also yellow.

Yellow is also the color of gold. George had several jewelry boxes loaded with gold cuff links and rings with Mercury's image, gold barefoot medallions, a few gold coins, gold chains, watches with yellow or gold bands, and water ski pins from around the world. It was a treasure trove of interesting memorabilia in gold and yellow.

Nutrition and Health

Bananas come in their own little yellow jacket and they're available all year round. According to George, bananas are the most perfect food. Each banana is loaded with nutrients and it's only about 100 calories.

"I've been into good food and exercise since I was a teenager," George told a *People* magazine reporter. "Good diet includes the banana because it has lots of vitamin B6 and vitamin C and a ton of potassium."

George banned white flour, refined sugar, and processed foods from his diet. He ate mostly vegetables, grains, and fish.

"Your body is your most valuable possession, but some people don't take care of their valuables," George said in an interview with *ESPN*. "When you stop to think about it—nothing else matters. You've got to feed it good food and keep it moving."

When the Blair girls were children, Halloween was one of the few times they were allowed candy—and even then, it was quite limited. Dorothy and the girls spent all day popping corn, filling up small, waxed-paper bags, and tying them with a ribbon to give out as treats. When the girls arrived home with bags of candy from trick-or-treating, George sifted through the piles and tossed most of the candy out. "We were allowed to keep the chewing gum," said GeeGee.

"'Pass the poison' was code for 'Pass the sugar,'" Robin recalled. "We did have raw brown sugar in the house, but we rarely used it!"

Despite the ban on refined sugar, George had a sweet tooth for homemade desserts and dark chocolate.

"I don't eat fast food, I don't drink sodas, and I don't eat cake. A dull, dreary, mundane, lousy existence you say—but wait a cotton-picking minute! If you could just peek over my shoulder at breakfast, you would see me zestfully attacking a Texas Ruby Red grapefruit one segment at a time until hardly anything is left except the rind, or reveling in each bite of a juicy, ripe melon, papaya, or mango. They are packed with vitamins and minerals."

George always kept a bowl of nuts on the counter for quick snacks. He believed that no one over the age of three should drink cow's milk.

George was not shy about sharing his thoughts on nutrition and the American diet. He had a genuine desire to help others lose weight and improve their eating habits.

"You know what I hate to see?" George told a *St. Petersburg Times* reporter. "I hate to see somebody drinking a sugary cola or eating something with white flour. Yuck. Everything should be whole-grain. I drink more plain water than any man in history. I'm really obnoxious about food. I think I'm right and everybody else is wrong."

The Cooper Institute and Clinic in Dallas, Texas, is the choice of many notables for annual physical exams. Dr. Kenneth Cooper is known around the world as the father of aerobics. At age eighty, George decided to find out what such a renowned physician would say about his fitness level. George was proud to say he was one of Cooper's "prize patients." Dr. Kenneth Cooper served as his medical advisor for many years.

When George's diet was evaluated, he was given an A+ by the clinic nutritionist. The doctors noted on his chart "appears younger than age." One year, Dr. Cooper wrote "considering the number of fractures in the back in the past year, I am amazed you continue to function as well as you do."

In 2006, Dr. Cooper wrote to George:

> It was great to see you again and be brought up to date regarding the phenomenal things you are doing past ninety years of age. Without question, your performances are "world class" and I continue to "tell your story" to people all over the world. Thanks so much for allowing me to introduce you to the class when I talk about aging properly. You are truly an example for all of us, and I wish you continued good health, good water skiing, and good snowboarding.

Grandson Oliver

Oliver remembers: "Sitting in the cafeteria at Shrewsbury Borough Grammar School, I was filled with a nervous excitement awaiting the arrival of my grandfather. Everyone in the third and fourth grades was there. They all knew my grandfather as a celebrity because I was not shy to brag about his accomplishments and he appeared in the *Scholastic News*. "He's the coolest!" "He drove a racecar!" "He's in the *Guinness*

Book of World Records!" "My grandfather was on *Oprah!*" This was the chance for all my claims of his superior awesomeness to be validated, hoping he would boast about his adventures, his travels, TV appearances, or tell us the secret to being the best at everything.

"He arrived, took the stage, and for the next thirty minutes, talked about nutrition to a group of seven-, eight-, and nine-year-olds who were used to their mothers cutting the crust off their white bread fluffernutter sandwiches, which they washed down with Yoo-hoo! His address was delivered extemporaneously but passionately; the importance of his message would become clear to me only later in life. At the time, I couldn't help but feel disappointed. He never mentioned racecars, meeting royalty, barefooting behind airplanes, or his appearance on television with Oprah. (They even hugged.)

"Instead of awesomeness, he called sugar 'poison' (gasp). He denounced white bread and encouraged whole wheat bread (yuck). He told us how many of the foods our generation was eating and loved were filling our bellies but starving us of nutrients; sugary breakfast cereal and fast food." He was one man waging war against processed foods, Agribusiness, and unhealthy school lunches. I felt the importance of his message was lost on us.

"I continued to sit in that cafeteria until I graduated from eighth grade in 2001, but I had a much better understanding of how being mindful of your intake will dictate the quality of your output. I was hoping my grandfather would detail why *he* was awesome; instead he told us how we're all able to be awesome. "You are what you eat. So, stop eating crap!"

The Doctor Who Became a Barefooter

Dr. Ted Eisenstat was impressed with George's health when he first met him as a seventy-two-year-old patient in New York City. "You look like you're in pretty good shape," he told George after giving him a full physical.

"Son, I'm in great shape. I'm the oldest barefoot water skier in the world!"

Dr. Eisenstat approved of George's nutritional regimen of a diet rich in fish, vegetables, and fruit—it was obviously working well.

It wasn't long before the doctor/patient relationship turned into a friendship. George taught Ted to barefoot water ski. Ted began attending the Blairfoot Bananza tournaments in Winter Haven and watching George perform in the Cypress Gardens shows.

During one of the shows, the performers were lined up on stage getting ready to take a bow when one of the clowns playfully pushed George into the water. George was not wearing his wetsuit at the time and he had negative buoyancy; he sank under the surface. He had nearly drowned three times as a child.

"He can't swim!" JoAnne screamed.

One of the performers quickly turned around, dove in, and brought George up to the surface.

Chapter 11
Around the World on Water Skis

JOANNE REMEMBERED: "GEORGE and I spent a lot of time traveling to visit the hospitals serviced by HPS. We had several hospitals in Puerto Rico and had driven pretty much all over the island. One of our main hospitals was San Juan Presbyterian where the newborn nursery was in the capable hands of Candy Marfisi. On this visit [in 1977], we were scheduled to meet with the administrator and some of the officers to go over a new contract. The administrator was called out of town on an emergency and was scheduled to return the following week. We looked at a map and realized that Colombia was fairly close. We'd never been there, so why not spend our unexpected free week seeing a new (to us) country?

"A couple of days later, we landed at the Cartagena airport where we rented a car and took off for Santa Marta, a small town on the Caribbean where we had heard there was water skiing. We didn't find a ski boat, but we did find someone with a flat rowboat who talked us into going to the jungle with him. In the jungle were many mango trees—mangos were one of George's very favorite fruits. He gorged on these tree-ripe mangos. As a result, he spent the remaining two days in Santa Marta close to the bathroom in our cottage. He had had a few too many ripe mangos.

"One week from the day we had landed in Cartagena, we were back in the airport, but with some additional luggage. On our way to the airport, we had passed a bar, and hanging near the doorway of the bar was a folk art painting. It made one happy just to look at it. George stopped the car. 'I've got to have that painting!' he proclaimed.

"We went into the bar and tried to bargain with the owner, who was not willing to part with his painting. Since we did not speak Spanish, we were at a big disadvantage. However, as usual, George prevailed. The painting (which measured 58" x 47" was strapped onto the top of our little Volkswagen; George gave the owner the full asking price: $25.00, and off we went.

"Our troubles were just beginning. We went up to the Avianca ticket desk, and George decided to go return the car while I took care of checking in. I propped our newly acquired painting against the counter and presented our tickets to the agent. 'What are you doing with that?' she asked.

"'We're taking it with us,' I replied. 'Where is the crate?' she asked. 'We don't have a crate—we'll just take it as is,' I replied.

"Oh, no you won't—it's against the rules." She called in some reinforcements. They all agreed that the painting could not go on the plane in its present state.

"At this point, George appeared. I had been wondering where he had disappeared to. He was accompanied by two policemen, one on each side. It turned out that there was no place in the airport to return the rental car and the police were arresting George. They thought he had stolen the car. When they saw me—I was distraught and did not appear to be a threat to anyone—they softened their attitudes somewhat. Plus, I showed them our international driver's licenses with our pictures on them. It seemed to make no difference that they had expired.

"In the end, we were allowed on the plane with the uncrated painting and George was not arrested.

"But then came the landing in Bogota. The flight had gone well—quite smooth and without incident. We glided down to the runway. George turned to me. 'Boy that was a really smooth landing!' he exclaimed. Suddenly, the plane fell onto its left side and stopped. The landing gear had collapsed and the wing was broken in half. George leaped over the seat in front of him, kicked out the emergency door, threw his jacket to me, who was behind him, and demanded, 'Follow me!'

"A male flight attendant tried to stop George but failed. George ran down the broken wing. Two attendants grabbed me and I couldn't pull away. All the passengers were held on the plane until a rope for everyone to hold on to was fastened in place. Meanwhile, a fire truck was brought into the field and was focused on the plane, making us fear the plane was about to catch fire.

"Finally, we were allowed off the plane. I had to find George. 'Yo estoy buscando a mi esposo,' ['I am looking for my husband'] I told everyone I saw. One policeman exclaimed, 'El está en la ambulancia' ['He's in the ambulance'] and pointed straight ahead. When I arrived at the ambulance, there was George, hooked up to an EKG. He looked at me and quietly gave the OK signal.

"'What could I do?' he asked me later. 'When I reached the bottom of the wing, there were two policemen waiting. If the police were arresting me in Cartagena for doing nothing, what would they do to me here, when I had knocked out the emergency door of the plane? So I feigned a heart attack.'

"The painting—which we love—hangs in our home. Many guests have asked where we found it. 'It's quite a story' is always the answer."

African Odyssey

(Written by George for *The Water Skier* magazine, July/August 1982)

"Who ever heard of taking a wetsuit on an African safari?" JoAnne asked George as they packed for their trip to Africa.

"You never know," I told her. "Africa's a big place, and if we're lucky, we just might find a barefoot oasis!"

"Well, I suppose Africa's as likely a place for barefooting as India was," JoAnne agreed. She was referring to my "find" of last year, Radia's Water Ski School on Chowpatty Beach in the heart of Bombay. Mr. Radia had been helpful and anxious for me to demonstrate barefooting before the crowds at Chowpatty. His ski boat really wasn't fast enough, and it was a struggle, but I managed to be the first barefooter to skim across the Bay of Bombay.

This year, JoAnne and I were headed for Gambia, West Africa, with a group of twelve avid bird watchers. Our trip to Gambia would last two weeks, and then JoAnne and I were going on alone to Nigeria and Kenya, and from there I was to travel to South Africa on business while she returned home.

A few days after our early December departure, our group was encamped in a beach hotel a few miles outside of Gambia's capital city of Banjul. Our trip to Banjul from Dakar (where our Pan Am flight landed) had been a bit arduous because of the heat, rough-surfaced roads, and a three-hour wait for the ferry to cross the Gambia River to Banjul. Nevertheless, we had been amused by seeing many monkeys along the route and had stopped several times to focus our binoculars on various species of African birds. JoAnne and I were rapidly getting into this new sport, but I always had one binocular lens on the lookout for a likely body of water for skiing.

And then it happened! Our first Saturday in Gambia, I heard about some skiers who met every weekend at the Denton Bridge, halfway between our hotel and Banjul.

JoAnne and I hopped into a taxi and off we went to Denton Bridge. There we found a happy group of skiers, among them Chris and Cathy White, from the English Medical Research Council, with their ski boat, Barbara Bruke from the American Embassy, and Pat and Tony Sparks. They generously offered to pull us (JoAnne with skis, me without). None of them had ever seen barefooting before and they were thrilled to watch the various starts and one-foots, and to be given some pointers on how to begin footin'. I, of course, couldn't believe my luck—barefooting in West Africa!

The following Monday, our group of bird watchers boarded the Lady Chilel, a working ship, to spend two days and nights traveling up the Gambia River with our binoculars and cameras. We stopped thirty times at outlying villages where frenzied loading, unloading, and trading of everything from salt to goats and peanuts was loaded on. Then a few nights of camping and we returned to Banjul in time for me to barefoot in a regatta that Sunday. Gambia had indeed turned out to be a barefooting oasis.

JoAnne and I stopped in Nigeria on HPS business, but we had no time for skiing, although I was promised a tow along the shores of Lago upon my return. From there we traveled to Nairobi, Kenya where we stayed at the historic Norfolk Hotel. This is the hotel from which Teddy Roosevelt set off on safari with 500 bearers in 1909.

Our first Kenyan safari was from Nairobi to the coastal town of Mombasa. On the way, we had three days of recording big game with a video camera. One night, while staying in a lodge at Tsavo East National Park, we were surprised to find a friendly elephant at our door paying us an evening visit!

Our hotel in Mombasa was right on the Indian Ocean and had advertised that water skiing was available. But one look at their boat and I knew it was hopeless, a 50-hp motor and choppy water to boot. Surely there was someplace to barefoot in this charming old seacoast town.

JoAnne and I hired a taxi and proceeded to the Bahari Deep Sea Fishing Club. No luck. No speedboats, too rough, and no one who knew anything about water skiing. Our defeat was visible as we returned to the taxi. When the driver questioned us, we told him our dilemma.

"Why didn't you tell me what you were looking for?" he asked. "I know where the water ski club is!" (How many times in our travels have we been saved by taxi drivers?)

He quickly drove us to a stately residential district, and sure enough, next to one of the houses, was a sign, "Mombasa Water Sports Club." At the end of a long flight of steps leading to an enclosed bay, we could see a boat equipped with 115-hp outboard motor. Soon we were introduced to Mr. Yusuf Mamujee, the boat's owner, and were involved once again in a friendship based on a love of water skiing. Yusuf is one of the few skiers on Africa's East Coast. He had never seen barefooting before, and his enthusiasm for this new form of skiing was boundless.

We spent the next several days in Mombasa sightseeing and skiing. Yusuf and his charming wife, Fiza, introduced us to many of their friends and we enjoyed a heart-warming Christmas season with them.

Several years ago, the *New York Times* published an article about an idyllic resort town north of Mombasa named Malindi. JoAnne had saved the article, which mentioned the Ocean Sports Hotel as a place where water skiing was offered. We decided to visit the hotel, so we rented a car and drove north out of Mombasa. Malindi has been "discovered" in the intervening years and is not quite as the *Times* writer had depicted it, but the Ocean Sports Hotel about ten miles south of town to Watamu is still a small, charming resort. And sure enough, water skiing was still available.

The ski boat had a 65-hp motor and the skiing was done right on the wavy Indian Ocean. Although I did manage to barefoot, it was rough so the conditions were far from optimum.

The scenery more than made up for the poor skiing, though, and we enjoyed our stay. The only problem was Watamu experienced a water shortage at the time, so the showers were only turned on for a short period each morning and evening. Finally, when the sea got rougher and the shower water became scarcer, JoAnne and I scurried back to Mombasa and the joys of friends, unlimited drinking water, and a well-equipped ski boat.

After all our fun and adventures in West and East Africa, I headed south for Cape Town while JoAnne returned home. Many travelers consider Cape Town to be one of the most beautiful cities in the world. To me, it seemed even more dramatic than San Francisco. The Atlantic Ocean there is crystal clear and beautiful blue in color, but I was surprised to find the water, even in the summer (November to May), so cold that it's impossible to swim.

Water skiers in this part of the world bypass the freezing water of the ocean for the warm water of Lake Zeekoi Vlei, only an hour from Cape Town. There I was the guest of Mark Jardine and Neil Hermann, South African barefoot trophy winners who are members of a ski club on the lake. Early each morning and late each afternoon, we enjoyed good footing.

It was difficult to leave such good times, but I had business in Johannesburg. For four days, I tried to obtain accommodations on the overnight "Blue Train" (often described as the most elite train in the world), but it was fully booked, and I eventually flew to "Joburg." A friend, Kevin Murphy from Australia, met me at the airport, and the next day he drove me to Vincent Wariner's Marine Store, where I found the most complete lineup of water skis and related equipment in Africa.

We picked up a gorgeous ski boat (with a 200-hp Mercury outboard motor) and off we went to the Eligwa Ski Club. Unfortunately, when we arrived, there was so much rain and wind that we were unable to ski. It reminded me of the bad weather at the 1981 Barefoot Nationals, but I was so hyped up that when the rain let up a little, I footed anyway.

The next day was a different story. We hit the warm and glassy water promptly at 6:30 a.m. For the next three-and-a-half hours, four of us took turns on the boom and long line, footing to our heart's content. By this time, the ski club and the river were bursting with activity.

The remainder of the day was an experience I'll not soon forget. Here was a ski club with about 125 family members, and nearly half of them had caravans (trailers) in place right on the shore of the river where the club owned 600 feet of frontage. All day there was activity with boats being launched, moving in and out from the dock, and skiers and barefooters taking off continually.

I was surprised to see the latest version of nearly every American ski and barefoot boat. Later in the day, we cruised a few miles up the Vaal River to where there was another ski club complete with a jump ramp and slalom course and with the same variety of modern ski boats.

The next morning, I flew to Durban. Vince told me that someone from their barefoot club would probably meet me at the airport. When I got off the plane and walked through the terminal, there were at least 100 people waiting to meet friends. By the time I reached the end of the line without anyone greeting me, I was feeling dejected. Just then, I spied a beautiful blonde who was holding a waterski magazine in front of her. A royal welcome was given me by no other than the women's barefoot champion of South Africa, Avril Tucker. She invited me to her ski club where I had the pleasure of footin' behind a boat owned by barefoot champion Mike Higgs, an inboard-outboard with about four inches of freeboard that threw a wake so low and round that, for the first time in my life, I accomplished several one-foot wake crossings.

The highlight of this portion of my barefoot odyssey was watching South African junior champion Dean Levy (just turned ten years old) do almost everything in the book with great skill. We wound up a fun day footing together.

My African journey ended the next day when I flew home to Red Bank, New Jersey, and sub-freezing temperatures. While it's always a pleasure to be home again, I missed the many friends and the good skiing I found while footin' my way across Africa.

86 *Banana George!*

Magazine covers featuring Banana George

Courtesy of USA Water Ski.

Photo credit: Martin Bydalek

Photo credit: Lynn Novakofski

Don't Wait for Life to Happen—Make it Happen 87

Banana George Living Life with Intensity at 80.

Armor All

SUPER STAR
Banana George Blair: Mr. Ambassador

Water Ski magazine April 1989 feature article by Terry Temple.
Photo credit: Tom King

Don't Wait for Life to Happen—Make it Happen

Banana George and David Letterman, 1992
Illustration by Mike Okamoto

Banana snowboarding, 1998
Illustration by Patrick Merewether

The Banana Snowboarding Team, George and his grandsons

Banana George shredding in Steamboat, Colorado

Don't Wait for Life to Happen—Make it Happen

Movie poster compliments of Bush Entertainment, John Biffar, CEO

Caption: *Top:* Banana George shaking hands with King Hussein of Jordan

George, Prince Albert of Monaco, and JoAnne Blair at the Grand Prix, 2000

George skiing on hydrofoils and Air Chair

Men's Health magazine, June 1998 "Live to 90 (and die having sex)"
Photo credit: Brian Smith

Banana George!

Top left: Tender Thoughts, *top right:* Leanin' Tree, *bottom:* OXO

Top: Diagram of the contoured Banana Cup
Bottom: George barefooting wearing the Banana Boa neck brace

Yellow wetsuit anyone?

Imprint of Banana George's feet at entrance to Lake Florence home, plus his signature pith helmets

Folk art painting from Colombia in George and JoAnne's Lake Florence kitchen

George playing the drums, 1994

Banana George in his custom pith helmet

George driving his Barefootin' Banana Boat III

George with his favorite feline named Hermes 2006

JoAnne and George 2010

Birthday celebration 2005, George conducts his family
Photo credit: Lynn Novakofski

George with great-granddaughters Jessica and Hayleigh Blair, 2006
Photo credit: Joseph DiOrio

George with great-grandsons Antonio and Nicholas Turrisi, 2006

USA Water Ski Hall of Fame look-a-likes

Phil Keoghan and Banana George

Ninetieth Birthday Celebration 2005 at Cypress Gardens with Aqua Maids Shaune Stoskopf and April Pear.
Photo credit: Lynn Novakofski

Hugs, JoAnne and George in New York City 2012

Kisses, George on a sit ski at 94 years old with Ashley Townsend and Barb Muren

Photo credit: Martin Bydalek

Section III
A New Focus

1985–2013
"A man who never quits is never defeated."
– "Banana" George Blair

CHAPTER 12

Florida to Antarctica to Russia with Love

GEORGE AND JOANNE were taking more and more trips to Florida so that George could ski in the Cypress Gardens Shows and continue to compete.

"I think it's time to sell HPS and move to Florida," George told JoAnne one day. "Donna will take care of Fogging Unlimited." The idea of a typical American retirement didn't appeal to him. He wanted to devote his time to promoting the sport of water skiing and barefooting.

George and JoAnne's next project was to find a house in Florida near Cypress Gardens. JoAnne said, "We were still busy with the company, but we went down to Winter Haven nearly every weekend. George would ski in the Cypress Gardens show while I looked at houses. George wanted a house on a lake, and he was looking for a lake that wasn't connected to the many channels in Florida to ensure less boat traffic."

Finally, one weekend JoAnne said to George, "I can adapt to anything. There are three houses to look at this weekend. I hope you'll like one of them, but if not, then you can take over the search." He looked at the first house and announced, "This is it!" Was it really "it," or did he just not want to take over? In any case, it proved to be a wonderful house for them and all their visitors and family for many years.

It was time to close one chapter and move on to the next. In 1985 George had received several offers for HPS, so he decided it was time to sell the company. It was sold to First Foto, the second largest (next to HPS) hospital baby photographers. The Red Bank office stayed open with GeeGee as the manager and most employees staying on.

The World Barefoot Tournament was being held in Australia in 1985, and George and JoAnne flew out to attend. On their way back home from Australia, they stopped in St. Louis where they met the First Foto executives and completed the deal to sell the company.

Soon after the trip, George and JoAnne settled into their home on Lake Florence, one mile from Cypress Gardens. They immediately began to customize every aspect of it. Eventually, the kitchen, the garage, the laundry/utility room, and bathrooms were painted in shades of yellow. In due course, the gray exterior of the house succumbed to the yellow fever. The front entrance landing was customized with Banana George's footprints and signature embedded in the concrete to greet you.

Upstairs, the spacious master suite included an office with windows overlooking the lake. George could monitor the wind conditions and activity on the water. His office was his command center. There he was surrounded by business and personal files, photos, memorabilia, notes, to-do lists, and frequently ringing telephones. It was the place for quiet discussions. Being summoned to his office could be daunting or a sweet time to share ideas.

George created a game and dorm room for when the house was overflowing. He wanted a place for his grandchildren and great-grandchildren to hang out and connect. He installed a pool table and a *Space Invaders* game. The pool table was also the base for a ping pong table whenever someone wanted to play. The custom-built game cabinets for chess, puzzles, and playing cards featured yellow banana-shaped pull handles.

Connected to that room was the trophy and memorabilia room, loaded with medals and trophies, a picture gallery, and a huge collage of many of the famous people George had met on his travels, including Brooke Shields, King Hussein of Jordan, Prince Albert of Monaco, Regis and Kathy Lee, Oprah, and David Letterman and many famous skiers and barefooters.

Tempo and Rhythm

The Music Room was complete with a bright yellow drum set, a piano, bongos, maracas, and tambourines. The grandkids would gather around George and spend hours dancing and making music together.

Grandson Oliver remembers: "At GB's house in Winter Haven, Florida, long days out on the water often concluded with music before or after dinner. As a youngster, I was inclined to dance to the music rather than play an instrument. You garner much more attention as a cute little kid when gyrating around in the center of the room while everyone else is sitting on the periphery.

"In between hip thrusts and arm waving, I loved to watch GB play drums, and I began to notice that when there was a drum solo, all the other musicians would stop, listen, and wait for him to finish before continuing.

"One morning, feeling restless, I went into the music room and climbed behind the drum set. Not yet big enough to reach all of the drums and pedals, I haphazardly tried out all of the sounds. With the gusto of a great conductor, I created a raucous cacophony, hitting the drums without rhythm or tempo in mind.

"GB marched out of his bedroom and looked over the balcony. 'What is that racket?' he asked. I remember him coming down and explaining to me how to play. "Walk your feet," he said. Those three words and a brief demonstration gave me the basis for almost everything played in 4/4 time; bass drum on one and three, hi-hat (or snare) on two and four. Playing the drums was about keeping time plus creating rhythms. The concept was over my head at the time, but the lesson was reinforced every time he played. As he steadily seesawed back and forth, I was mesmerized by how his hands fluttered with different rhythms and his feet consistently kept the tempo. That was my first drum lesson, and I know I'm part of his tradition every time I play."

Mercury/Lithophanes

Around this time, George's collection of Roman god Mercury/Hermes art objects began to grow. His interest in Mercury began when he was a boy in the 1920s and visiting his Uncle Ira's film developing darkroom. At the entrance to this magical room was a statue of Mercury. George was given that statue after Uncle Ira's death, and he cherished it.

George's older brother Laurel, a world traveler and art collector, is credited with getting George to start a Mercury collection. George had sculptures life-size to miniature, lithographs, paintings, tapestries, cuff links, rings, and ceramics representing the Roman god who was "fleet of foot." Mercury was known as the god of commerce and travel. Hermes was his Greek counterpart. The more George learned about this messenger of the gods, the more drawn he was to him as his alter ego. He even named one of his cats "Hermes." George's collection was fascinating and vast. For a while, he even had a gold-plated Mercury ornament on the hood of his, guess what, yellow Lincoln Mark VIII, or was it the yellow Cadillac? It later became illegal to have hood ornaments so it had to go!

Laurel founded The Blair Museum of Lithophanes located in Toledo, Ohio. Lithophanes are three-dimensional translucent porcelain plaques that, when backlit, reveal detailed magical images. They were first created in Europe in the 1820s. The Blair Museum has the largest collection in the world. After his dear brother's death, George continued to be active with the museum and one of its most generous donors: www.lithophanemuseum.org.

World Water Ski Tournament

George was invited to attend the 1986 World Water Ski Tournament in Germany along with the US team as a supporter (he was a generous donor) and as an exhibition skier.

For the opening ceremony, Franz Kirsch, organizer of the tournament, had arranged for the German water ski team to erect a large paper sign in front of the jump. George was on a long line behind the boat, and at the last minute, he cut hard to go over the jump and exploded through the paper. The crowd gasped in surprise and delight—not only at the novelty of his entrance but also at the fact that a seventy-five-year-old guy went over the jump. The average barefoot water skier often stopped jumping in his or her forties.

"George was a happy-go-lucky fella," said William Farrell, the team captain. "He wasn't a daredevil to us, but he seemed like a daredevil to others. His focus was on the positive and good things. Because of him, we kept developing new divisions in barefoot competitions. He was generous in many different ways and provided financial support for the teams." The synergy at the tournament was high and George's enthusiasm pulled them along. The United States team won the Gold Medal, Australia was second and Great Britain third out of fourteen countries.

The Quest of the Last Continent, Antarctica

In 1986, George decided to go, of all places, to Antarctica. Joanne recalls how the decision was made:

"George and I were sitting in our Florida living room chatting with my brother Jimmy and sister-in-law Shirley. We were discussing our various travels. Suddenly, Jimmy turned to George and said, 'Do you realize that you've skied on all the continents except one?'

"'Oh, no!' George was incredulous. 'Which one did I miss?'

"'Antarctica!' said Jimmy.

"George's next words could have been predicted by anyone who knew him well. 'I have to do something about this,'" George said. He turned to me and said, 'Who do I call to arrange a trip to Antarctica?'

George spent the next nine months putting the plans in place. When he called the travel agent to arrange the trip, the agent was dubious at first. Water skiing in Antarctica? On bare feet?

From his notes, George recalled the planning that took place:

> There is nothing I like more than a challenge, so I immediately started to find out how I could arrange it. I found out that Lindblad Expeditions was planning a trip, so I got in touch with them and told them what I wanted to accomplish. At first, they were totally unbelieving that I was serious, but I finally convinced them.
>
> Then I called my eldest grandson, Robbie, and asked him how he would like to have, as a present for his college graduation, a trip to Antarctica. At first, he thought I was joking, but then he picked up my vibes of excitement and confidence and he embraced it 100 percent.

Less than a year earlier, the Antarctica weather station had recorded earth's lowest temperature ever: a mind-blowing -129°. It would take a Herculean effort to coordinate and plan the entire excursion. But as you know by now, George always loved a challenge, so he persisted with the quest. The agent booked George and Robbie on the *M. S. Explorer* cruise ship. George arranged for a crew from *The Today Show* to film his adventure.

The plane touched down at 11:30 p.m. with plenty of daylight left. At the earth's southernmost tip, the summer days were long and the nights were short. Sundown commenced at 1 a.m. and the sun rose again just two hours later.

George and Robbie's destination was Deception Island. It is surrounded by a submerged volcano and home to thirty summer-based scientific research bases from several countries. In 1967 and 1969, two of the research facilities were destroyed by molten mud. *M. S. Explorer* anchored near Deception Island in Bransfield Strait.

"It was cold, but it was beautiful at the south tip of the world," George told a reporter. "The land around the bay was black volcanic rock. I had never seen anything quite like it."

In his diary, January 8, 1986, George recorded:

> After Robbie and I had flown to Rio de Janeiro and to Buenos Aires and then to the southernmost tip of Argentina, we saw the ship that would carry us the rest of the way. When I walked up to the top of the gang plank, the captain said, "Welcome aboard, Banana George!" He said, "I want you to know that every officer and crewman is dedicated to helping you pull off your mission." He said, "I'd like you to go up to the bow deck and see what I've got for you."
>
> Well, I ran up there with Robbie and we saw the prettiest little 15' boat with a 150-horsepower Mercury outboard engine and a ski-tow pylon. I ran back to the captain and said, "Where did you get such a nice ski boat?" He said, "I had to go all the way to Singapore!"

The smiling crew greeted George and Robbie with a silver tray of gin and tonic drinks. In no time at all, George had everyone singing until the wee hours of the morning.

The next day the crew from the *Explorer* lowered the ski boat into the calm bay. A thermometer dipped into the water registered 28°. "A little chilly!" George laughed. He was dressed in a drysuit with a neoprene hat.

The historic run was logged in the captain's book: "Today, we met our first iceberg, saw our first humpback whale…and Mr. George Blair performed his barefoot water skiing along the beach."

George won a spot in the 1988 *Guinness Book of World Records* as the only man who barefoot water skied on all seven continents.

Second Broken Back—1987

At seventy-two, George was practicing his barefoot jumping at Lake Florence one morning. On his first jump, he rocketed off the ramp and landed at what he estimated was a personal best jump of forty feet. His previous record was set at thirty-four feet. George was euphoric when he approached the ramp again. This time he wasn't concentrating. His knees buckled, causing him to hit the ramp with his tailbone instead.

"I knew I had broken my back," George told a Montreal reporter. "I was in mortal pain. I thought I was going to die." The X-rays showed a fracture on the L3 vertebra.

"You'll need to stop barefooting until you have a complete recovery," the doctor told George. "This could take two to three months."

George mentally calculated his recovery time and realized it would fall around the same time he was scheduled to do a filming for *The Guinness Book of World Records*. There was no way he was going to miss this opportunity since it had taken months to set it up.

"My family, friends, and doctors advised me to cancel that date, and I promised I would if I wasn't recovered," George said.

Eleven weeks after the back-breaking incident, George was footing and smiling into the cameras. "My confidence never wavered and the date was kept—the show was televised in thirty-three countries and replayed countless times."

Russia 1988

On February 13, 1988, the Blairs were reading through the *New York Times* when they came across an article about Viktor G. Afanasyev, the editor of *Pravda*, a Russian newspaper. The article mentioned that Viktor was an avid water skier.

"I wonder if I could barefoot in Russia," George mused. The idea of being the first water skier from America to ski behind the Iron Curtain intrigued George. JoAnne crafted a letter to Viktor.

"We were particularly delighted to learn that you are an avid water skier," she wrote. "My husband, George, is also an avid water skier, in the barefoot category. As you can see by the enclosed articles, he is very active in competitive barefoot skiing here in the States and has been named the United States Ambassador for Barefoot Skiing. He has barefooted on all seven continents, but never in the USSR."

Weeks went by, and there was no response. Meanwhile, George began connecting with other Russian water skiers and sending letters to get to know them. At first, the letters he received were not optimistic about the idea of an American coming to Russia to exhibit in their shows. The Iron Curtain was solidly up, and the Russian view of Americans was negative. George did not give up. He continued to network with one person after another, convincing some friends to write letters on his behalf and to vouch for his sincerity. After many faxes and letters, the permission finally came: Not only could George exhibit his barefooting abilities during the water ski tournament in Moscow, but he was invited to the Friendship Tournament in Sofia, Bulgaria, and to water ski at Yalta on the Black Sea.

George recalled the first part of the trip, a visit to Sofia, Bulgaria, as follows:

> "There they are!"
>
> JoAnne and I looked at each other in relief as we heard Ralph Meloon's voice booming above the crowd at the airport in Sofia, Bulgaria. It was a hot day in August and we had just landed. The Friendship Cup Tournament in Sofia was my first stop on a trip I had long looked forward to. I still couldn't believe I had the good luck to be the first barefooter from the West to be invited to the Eastern Bloc. The Friendship tournament would welcome skiers from the USSR, East Germany, and Czechoslovakia.
>
> I brought a teaching boom with me as I hoped to provide some barefoot instruction along the way. My big hope was that this trip would introduce barefooting to many people who had never seen it before and it would engender enthusiasm for the sport in the Eastern Bloc countries.

Ralph Meloon, head of the Correct Craft Boat Company, was the force behind this Bulgarian section of the trip. He brought a group of skiers to the airport and they presented JoAnne with a beautiful bouquet of roses, the national flower of Bulgaria. We climbed into the van, which was reserved for our use during the tournament, and met our interpreter, Yao.

As soon as we dropped our luggage at the hotel, we took a sightseeing trip out to the site. It was about a half hour from the hotel and a perfect place for the tournament—with calm water, trees for shade, and bleachers for good viewing. Yao, who was not only our interpreter but also our guide for our stay in Sofia, showed us the cottage where we could rest during the tournament.

"We thought you might want to rest sometimes," he said. This was just one indication of the thoughtfulness of our hosts. They did everything possible to make us comfortable and ensure our stay was a happy one.

That evening, we joined Ralph, his wife Betty, and their granddaughter, Tanya, for dinner at the Bulgarian restaurant at our hotel. At that point, my pressing problem was the lack of bananas in Bulgaria. The Dollar store in the hotel had a very large poster advertising bananas at the front door, but there were none inside. (Dollar stores are scattered throughout Eastern Bloc countries and sell their goods only for hard currency—dollars, Deutsch marks, etc.)

The absence of bananas turned out to be a sad fact of life while we were in Sofia. Despite this great void, the tournament was otherwise very successful.

JoAnne recalls the next leg of the trip:

We headed for our next stop the following morning: Moscow. It was an exciting day—seeing the Russian capital for the first time. Red Square is so impressive—we enjoyed our tourist day, but left the next morning for Yalta on the Black Sea. As soon as we arrived and secured a room, George started the search for a barefoot boat. We made friends with an unsuspecting man who was lounging on a bench near the water. From what we could understand, he was the owner of a boat that was "high up" on a pulley. As soon as he had a little lunch, he would get the boat down for us.

Taking advantage of the wait time, we visited the site of the Yalta Conference, the famous meeting of Roosevelt, Churchill, and Stalin after World War II. After that, we had a visit to the home of the famous author Anton Chekhov.

When we arrived back at waterside, two men were waiting to bring the boat down. We all watched as it was slowly descending. It was a straightforward wooden boat, about nineteen feet—the size of a ski boat. We then started to notice the sky changing to a dark forbidding scene. The men quickly pushed the boat into the threatening sea. We motored slowly out and George took the ski handle. We took off and I nearly went overboard. It was more than rough—it was violent. The second man on board pushed me down on the floor of the boat and held me there. Even so, it was impossible to stay still and I had several cuts. We had to quit, but George had managed to get up on his feet and barefoot for several seconds—maybe even a minute. I was so preoccupied with trying to stay in the boat that I couldn't concentrate on anything else.

After Yalta came St. Petersburg, known to be one of the most beautiful cities in the world and the second largest in Russia. We visited the huge Hermitage museum with all its treasures. When we went back to our hotel, I received a call from my brother in Louisiana. My mother was in the hospital in intensive care.

I managed to get on a plane that day, stopped in Paris for one night at our apartment, took a plane to New York, and then another one to Louisiana. My mother pulled through.

The Eastern Bloc Ski Tournament was a wonderful affair. George received numerous accolades and press coverage. He also taught barefooting to many dedicated skiers, including young teens, so he felt he had accomplished his goal of introducing barefooting to the Eastern Bloc countries. The media went into a frenzy during George's visit and he made appearances on Soviet TV and in countless articles in newspapers. More importantly, George and JoAnne became instant friends with the Russian water ski team members. Before they left, George vowed to bring the Russians to America the following year.

"I hope that the people in the Soviet Union and in all the other countries of the world where I have gone, develop this interesting sport," George told a reporter. He later told David Letterman on *The Late Show* that in Russia they called him "Mr. Banana."

In 1995 George arranged for six members of the Russian ski team to come to America to train at Cypress Gardens with MasterCraft as a sponsor. When they arrived in New York City, JoAnne arranged for a big dinner at their apartment—forty-two people crammed around various tables to welcome the Russians. The next day, they flew to Florida to begin their training at Cypress Gardens. Four skiers competed at the Coors Light Pro Water Ski tour, becoming the first Russians to compete in an American tournament.

One of the skiers, Olga Gubarenko, a European silver medalist, injured her knee. George arranged for a local orthopedic doctor to craft a customized knee brace. Olga went back to Russia with the knee brace and wore it at a competition in France. She struggled in tricks and slalom, but to her surprise, she set a new national record in jumping.

"Thank you very much for my new national record in jumping," Olga wrote to George after the event. "It happened only due to your knee brace. After the surgeon told me about my torn ligament, I didn't believe I could jump forty meters. It was my great dream to jump forty meters and to do it [as] the first in our country. I'm very grateful to you."

In another letter, Olga reflected on her experience in the United States:

> I've heard many times before about USA, but only after this visit I understood that it was quite a different country from all others. The country and the people are the nicest of any country I have ever visited. We had really fantastic time. It seems to me that the American people is close to Russian people and it's beautiful.

The Russian team made a total of three trips to America, truly exhibiting friendship across the borders.

Chapter 13

Barefooting in Finland and Switzerland

"This is my chance!" George exclaimed.

"Your chance for what?" JoAnne asked.

As usual, she didn't know what to expect. Life with George was always an adventure, always unpredictable.

"The World Games are in Lahti, Finland this year, and I've been invited to give exhibitions. This is the perfect time for me to barefoot in the Arctic Circle!"

After barefooting in the southern-most cold waters of Antarctica, George figured it was only logical to add the goal of barefooting in the North Pole region. The two of them pulled out an atlas and looked up Lahti, located fifty miles north of Helsinki. Much further north in Lapland was the town of Rovaniemi, known as the City on the Arctic Circle—the home of St. Nicholas.

"It all seems fascinating, exotic, and *cold*," JoAnne said. "It's probably easier to find dogsled teams than barefooters up there!"

The director of the World Games directed them to the Pokka brothers, Finland's top two barefoot water skiers who happened to live in Lapland. "Bring your drysuit," they said. The plans moved forward quickly and the Blairs arrived in Rovaniemi to find the sun shining, the temperatures balmy, and the tourists in shorts!

After a quick bowl of reindeer soup at the hotel, the Pokka brothers arrived. Ari and Arto greeted the Blairs with enthusiastic hugs. "We are so happy you came to Lapland to barefoot! You are the reason we are barefooting. We saw you on TV seven years ago, in a program from Paris. After that, we built our own boat, with a boom and everything. We've been barefooting for four years!"

They all piled into the Pokka brothers' car with the ski boat hitched behind and took off for the Pokkas' summer cottage. Just fifteen minutes later, they slowed down to gaze at three reindeer on the side of the road.

"They are a menace here," Ari said. "The other day, there was a big pile up of cars because someone hit two reindeer." George and JoAnne were still thrilled to see Christmastime animals in their natural habitat.

As soon as they launched the boat, George was ready to ski. While Ari drove, Arto captured footage of George barefooting exuberantly across the lake doing all of his usual tricks.

When it was Ari and Arto's turn, the Blairs were amazed at their level of skill; they each took turns barefooting forward and backward, with several high-level tricks tossed in.

"How can you both be such good barefooters when you live in such a cold climate and have such a short season to practice?" George asked.

"We love the sport. And surprisingly enough, ice hockey helps us to train for barefooting because you have to keep the balance in the same way when you are wearing skates as when you are barefooting."

After skiing, the guys headed into the sauna. A few minutes later, several howls were emitted. It was customary practice for the Pokka brothers to acclimate Finland newcomers with a dose of ice-cold water!

In one of her articles, JoAnne described the rest of the trip:

> Our hotel room was very large, comfortable, and typically Finnish. The built-in cupboards and drawers were made of beautiful wood, fitted perfectly, and were a model of woodcarving. There were no black-out blinds, and while it was rather like twilight at 1:30 a.m., the sun never really disappeared.
>
> The next morning, Ari and Arto arrived and we drove to the lake on the Arctic Circle. This was another idyllic spot, bordered by strawberry fields and charming cottages. We launched the boat and George donned his drysuit. He finally accomplished his goal of barefooting across the famous Arctic Circle—under much warmer conditions than he ever imagined!

Ari and Arto left us around noon. They were both entered in the barefoot event at the World Games in Lahti, so they had to drive to their home in Tornio to pack and get on the road. George and I spent the afternoon with Tauno Romppaine, the videographer who captured George's Arctic run. He and his wife did their best to show us the main sights of Rovaniemi. It is a charming little town with pedestrian malls and the largest supermarket in Lapland—where we bought a box of what we hoped was hot rye cereal.

A visit to the Reindeer Farm found nearly all the reindeer hiding from the heat. Our hosts told us about the Annual Mosquito Hunt: one day a year, all the participants kill mosquitoes and there are prizes awarded for the largest mosquitoes killed. We were lucky—there were no mosquitoes in sight during our visit!

The highlight of the afternoon was our visit to St. Nicholas in his complex outside Rovaniemi. St. Nicholas truly has a perfect place to carry on his goal of making all children everywhere happy for Christmas. His post office is filled with bags of mail from all points of the globe. He has a large staff of helpers working in the post office. Mail pours in all through the year, and it takes many elves to see that it is all answered.

When we visited St. Nicholas in his splendid office, we could see why his special rocking chair in the post office is extra-sized. St. Nicholas is a very imposing figure—about 6' 8" tall. He, of course, speaks many languages and happily welcomes children of all nationalities every day. His helpers stand by with a digital camera to take pictures of his guests.

As we stood at the gate waiting for our plane back to Helsinki, a rather rugged-looking young man swooped down on us.

"Hey! Aren't you Banana George? What are you doing up here?"

"Barefooting across the Arctic Circle; what else?" George replied.

"Man, that's cool!"

"True—but not as 'cool' as I expected!"

Miss Switzerland and a Few Bananas

George and JoAnne were in Geneva, Switzerland, for the Fiftieth Anniversary Celebration of the International Waterski Federation. All went well and they were happy to be with many good friends, including Kuno Ritchard, president of the Federation.

The host hotel was the International Hilton. On the evening of the awards banquet, George and JoAnne sat with their good friend, Alain Zrihen from France. "George was always open to new opportunities; that is what helped make him successful. When he believed in something, it was difficult to change his mind, and that was a strength. George had a strong personality which blended with kindness—he was kind, happy, and always smiling," said Alain. As the evening wore on with one award after another, followed by one long speech after another, JoAnne whispered that she was exhausted and was going to head back to the hotel room to retire for the night.

The next morning, JoAnne opened the door to the hall and there was the Geneva morning paper…with a big picture of George on the front page handing out bananas to the newly crowned Miss Switzerland! It seems that after the banquet, Alain had informed George that something interesting was happening on another floor and wouldn't George like to investigate?

The two of them then picked up a couple of boxes of bananas left over from the banquet, descended to the fourth floor, and entered an auditorium where a ceremony to choose "Miss Switzerland" was taking place. Alain talked his way in, accompanied by George. Once they were in, Alain walked up on the stage. "Ladies and gentlemen," he announced, "I'd like to introduce world famous Banana George! We are here for the fiftieth anniversary of water skiing, and this man is important in history: he is the oldest barefoot water skier in the world!"

George bowed. Then he gave each stunned beauty contestant a banana and a kiss. The women couldn't help but laugh and smile at the exuberant George. When he stopped in front of the newly-crowned Miss Switzerland, he bowed and produced an entire cluster of bananas for her. The photographers went crazy.

That is how Banana George made the front page of Geneva's newspaper, *Le Matin*!

CHAPTER 14

Becoming a Hall-of-Famer

GEORGE WAS AN excellent role model for those on the second half of their life journeys because he constantly showed an alternative way to approach the aging process. With proper diet, exercise, and a "can do" attitude, George proved that senior citizens do not have to resign themselves to slowing down. As George said, "I don't need mountains. I make my own and then I climb them." In 1993, he told a reporter for the *Chicago Tribune*, "I go skiing with guys twenty or thirty years old and they get tired before I do."

He was as excited as a seven-year-old to get up every day and go to work or play with his friends. The spark of his intelligence and incredible health and vigor resulted in a personality that said every day, "I've got places to go and people to meet."

As Robin illustrates, "After a ski show at Cypress Gardens, some of the skiers come out in costume to greet the audience. One such time when we were visiting, an older woman in a wheelchair and her family were clamoring to see Banana up close. When the show announcer said that Banana was eighty years old, they could not believe that. Their faces showed disbelief in meeting him! The woman asked whether she could touch him for 'good luck,' and when she felt his bicep, she exclaimed, 'That is like a rock.' Meeting Dad was clearly amazing to her. I bet Dad was hoping he would inspire her to try to overcome the wheelchair as her family wheeled her away. Dad said, 'Ski ya later.'"

Don Buffa, Cypress Gardens, remembers George saying, "You have a short time on earth. Grab as much of life as you can."

In the summer of 1990, *Newsday* published an article called "Circle of Caring," which rankled George enough to write a letter to the editor.

> Dear Virginia:
>
> The "Circle of Caring" piece by Eda LeShan in *Newsday* is a morbid outlook for aging.
>
> I take issue with this statement, "By the time we are 60, I think we are just beginning to move toward a much smaller circle of caring. We tire more easily, we find traveling difficult...."
>
> To refute this outlook, let me give you an example of my activity at almost seventy-six years young.
>
> This past summer (1990), as a national champion barefoot water skier, I did performances in eleven different cities in Florida, Texas, California, New York, and Massachusetts. I competed in four barefoot tournaments, culminating at the National Tournament where I was awarded a first place in jumping, second in tricks, and third in slalom.
>
> During this time, I participated in sixteen different TV shoots throughout the country, twenty radio programs, and sixteen newspaper or magazine interviews.
>
> This morning, I was up at 6:45 to pack for a ten-day trip. I had a meeting at 10 a.m., then left for the Orlando airport where I took a plane to New York City. Tomorrow, I will drive to Shrewsbury, New Jersey, for the monthly meeting of the Board of Directors of Shrewsbury State Bank, of which I am a founder.
>
> The next day, I will fly to Phoenix where I will learn to barefoot around the corners of a new cable skiway. Then I will drive three hours to my home in California on the Colorado River.
>
> The next morning, I will assist several other water skiers in showing 230 handicapped children how to have fun on the water, including skiing, and put on a ski show for them. There will be a photo shoot on the river, featuring hotdog hydrofoilers and other antics.

Wednesday, I will drive back to Phoenix for a photo shoot on the new Phoenix Cable Skiway and then fly back to Florida. The following weekend will be devoted to entertaining the barefoot team from New Zealand that is in Winter Haven.

The week of the World Tournament, I will be in Jacksonville, Florida, doing barefoot exhibitions in three ski shows.

The following week will be for planning the annual "Blairfoot Bananza," which is primarily a barefoot endurance contest of which I have historically been one of the top contenders.

At seventy-five-plus, I have a huge and ever-expanding circle of caring friends. I am traveling more than ever before—approaching 100,000 miles per year. I have worked hard and played hard all my life, but I've never had more fun than I'm having right now!

Sincerely yours,
George A. Blair (Banana George)

Banana Claus

To the delight of audiences, George created a "Banana Claus" ski act for the Cypress Gardens holiday shows. Dressed in a spectacular yellow Santa Claus suit, he skied on hydrofoils around the show circle to the sound of Christmas music. Sometimes he was accompanied by the youngest skier to perform in the show, Parks Bonifay, whose parents were champion skiers and part of the show team for many years.

George's Attitude

JoAnne's brother, Jim White, recalled an incident that exemplified George's positive attitude:

> For a number of years, my wife Shirley and I celebrated Thanksgiving with JoAnne and George in either New York City or Florida. This year, the celebration would be in Florida.

Prior to our arrival from Louisiana, George had a fall while skiing and he fractured a vertebra. He was confined to a hospital bed in a downstairs bedroom. We thought we needed to cancel our trip, but George insisted we come. Two other guests had been invited, and George didn't want anyone to change plans.

The two other guests were Claudine and Yvan Godard. They have a house in Winter Haven and a home in Vierzon, France. Every summer, they sponsor a water ski show in Vierzon which is famous and well-attended. George had skied in Claudine and Yvan's show several times and he and JoAnne had become their good friends and skiing companions.

On Thanksgiving Day, we were gathered in the kitchen as JoAnne was finishing the last minute touches for her dinner. We were discussing how to prepare our plates and then all go into the room with George so he could be part of the festivities.

As the discussion was coming to a conclusion, George entered the kitchen dressed in a yellow tuxedo, yellow shirt, yellow shoes, and a yellow tie, announcing that he was ready for dinner. He proceeded to the dining room and sat down in his usual place at the head of the table. After we all wiped the stunned looks off our faces, the table was quickly set and dinner was served.

The meal was delicious and George was his usual effusive host. "Claudine and Yvan had never been to an American Thanksgiving dinner before. They loved it," said JoAnne. Had we not known about George's back and the severe pain he was in, no one would have been able to tell that anything was out of order.

George demonstrated to all of us that day how true strength looks. It was how he lived his life each and every day. Things happen. We choose how we will respond. George's response was always to overcome life's obstacles and to "Do It." He was an amazing man—and we are thankful to have been part of his family.

JoAnne's sister-in-law, Shirley White, remembers:

> When I think back over my years of knowing and loving George (AKA the "Banana Man"), so many memories come to mind: his energy, his positive attitude, his love of barefooting, his wonderful generosity with family and friends. Yet it was the quiet, tender side of George that many never saw that defined George for me.
>
> I remember so clearly the time George, JoAnne, Jim (JoAnne's brother), and I met in Meridian, Mississippi to attend a family wedding. JoAnne loves old carousels, and we heard about a turn-of-the-century carousel ride in the park in Meridian. It seemed like a fun way to spend a couple of hours, and off we went.
>
> The four of us thoroughly enjoyed our ride. As we rode, we noticed several children standing by the carousel watching us. Their clothing and shoes appeared very worn. They were looking longingly at the carousel.
>
> When the ride was over, the four of us walked back to the car to return to our hotel; then there were only three of us. George was missing! We started looking for George and found him at the carousel surrounded by the same four children. They were at the concession stand enjoying cotton candy, drinks, and each one had a carousel ticket. I will always remember their faces as they looked up at this man in all yellow. It was that day that George became a real hero in my heart and mind.
>
> When George looked at these children, he saw an opportunity to make someone's life just a little sweeter. I must admit that from that day on, when I looked at George, I saw a different man than the "celebrity." I saw a man with a tremendous heart.

Water Ski Hall of Fame 1991

One of the greatest honors a skier can receive is to be inducted into the Water Ski Hall of Fame in Polk City, Florida. In 1991, George was over-the-top when he was asked. Four generations of Blairs, all dressed in yellow, were there to watch George accept this esteemed honor. The Hall of Fame represented the best of the best in the sport. George would be listed among other great skiers such as Richard Pope, Sr., founder of Cypress Gardens (1982) and Brenda Nichols Baldwin (2017). In the beautiful exhibit hall would be his story, along with his portrait painted by famous skiing ballerina, Willa Cook, who was also inducted (1982). A life-size statue cast of his body barefooting in a toe-hold was the centerpiece. It was a weekend of celebrating with champagne, family, friends, and lots of skiing.

Unknown to George, his grandson Robbie had been planning a surprise to coincide with the whole family gathering to celebrate George's induction. Robbie recalled:

> While growing up, I perceived my grandfather as a serious guy who expected perfection. He was larger than life, and sometimes his approach was a little scary. I always tried to do the best I possibly could and hoped that it would meet his expectations.
>
> I was twelve when I tried barefooting for the first time. I was a natural at it, maybe because I had watched my grandfather and other barefooters so many times. We bonded over the sport.
>
> Later, we met in the morning and drove the boat for each other before going to work. I began competing in ski tournaments and developed a passion for trick skiing.
>
> Our relationship became a close one. After I got married, my wife and I had two daughters. I turned to George for advice in many areas of my life. He taught me to create opportunities and encouraged me by saying, 'You can do it, too.' I try to do the same thing for my girls—I emphasize to them that they can do anything they set their minds to. My grandfather believed that women should have equal opportunities.
>
> In many ways, my grandfather had become the father I longed for. He gave me the attention, guidance, and companionship I needed. I wanted to honor our relationship in a special way.

GB, I have something I want to tell you. You've been more than a grandfather to me; you've also been a father. To honor you, I have changed my last name to Blair.

George was so moved by Robbie's speech that he wept openly; it was a truly tender moment between them.

Banana Fan Clan

About this time, the Banana Fan Clan started a newsletter called *Going Bananas*. GeeGee and JoAnne co-wrote it, and then GeeGee designed, printed, and mailed it. This was before Facebook made it easy for people to keep up with Banana George's activities, so the newsletter shared his various trips, honors, and words of wisdom and inspiration on life, aging, and being active.

George constantly received cards, letters, and emails with requests for his autographed picture, his movie (see Chapter 15), or just words of encouragement to someone who needed it or was disabled. Here is a sample of a Christmas request he got in December 2000 from a fan in Minnesota.

> Dear Banana George,
>
> My husband, Bob, is an avid barefoot water skier and fan of yours. We recently saw you at the Denver airport. It was a highlight of our trip. I would like to order your movie video and the magazine reprint article for my husband for Christmas. Would you also be able to send me an autographed picture of yourself barefooting? I would greatly appreciate it.
>
> Thank you and have a great Christmas,
>
> Lynne Bunchek

Throughout their marriage, JoAnne personified the saying, "Behind every successful man there is a woman." Her administrative skills were invaluable in responding to the media, making travel plans, and answering requests and correspondence. George traveled often and also conducted business wherever he went. He had limited time to answer fan mail. JoAnne was a perfect partner with her cheery disposition and absolute support of all his crazy schemes and antics.

JoAnne was a proficient boat driver, for a very demanding skier. She was also a gracious hostess, adept at putting together spontaneous dinner parties. George was a magnet; people wanted to be around him and ski with him.

For instance, one day the doorbell rang. An English family had gotten Banana George's address from Cypress Gardens. They wanted to take a photo with him and get his autograph. George insisted they come in, go for a boat ride, and receive a ski lesson. He was spontaneous, loved his fans, and was more than accommodating to his admirers.

At their Lake Florence home, George and JoAnne would often host entire ski teams such as the Chinese, Japanese, Russian, Australian, German, French, New Zealander, and British teams. Their dear friend Kuno Ritchard, later the president of the International Waterski and Wakeboard Federation, was a favorite house guest.

"I believe there is nothing more important in life than what we leave behind in terms of how we have helped others. What will last in this world is what kind of influence we have had on others."

— Joe Gibbs, Pro Football Hall of Fame

Chapter 15

Daredevil and Movie Star

In 1994, the Captain of the Air Wisconsin flight from Sioux Falls, North Dakota, was carefully going through the checklist when the flight attendant informed him they were waiting for one more passenger to board. The flight was full—ninety-nine passengers—and there was just a single seat left. In just twelve minutes, the plane was scheduled to take off.

"He's a guy dressed in all yellow from head to toe, carrying a yellow briefcase," she said.

Captain Gordy Anderson's ears perked up. There could only be one passenger fitting that description: Banana George. Earlier that morning, Gordy had read an article about George in the Sioux Falls newspaper. As an avid water skier and barefooter, he was familiar with George and the sport.

"That's Banana George! When he boards, please direct him to the cockpit," Gordy instructed. "I'd like to meet him."

Minutes later, George burst into the cockpit in a yellow blur, exclaiming, "Good morning, Captain!" With a big smile, he extended a handshake to everyone while Gordy explained a bit of George's water skiing background to the copilot and flight attendant.

"Did you happen to see the MTV video featuring the World Champion Mike Seipel barefoot water skiing behind a seaplane?" Gordy then asked George.

"Yes! I called Mike and said that was the coolest thing I ever saw!"

"Well, I was the pilot for that one," Gordy grinned.

"You were flying it?" George's eyes grew wide.

"I sure was! How much layover time do you have in Chicago? I'll walk with you to your gate and we can talk more."

After they landed, the two men chatted as they walked through the O'Hare tunnel from Terminal B to C. As they boarded the moving walkway, fans recognized George easily.

"Hey, George. I saw you snowboarding in Steamboat Springs [Colorado]!"

"Hi, George. I saw you ski at Cypress Gardens!"

A few young women blew George kisses. Several people reached over the railing to grab a quick handshake. When George and Gordy arrived at the gate, a small crowd gathered around George. Gordy waited patiently as George showered attention on every fan and handed out his cards.

Finally, the two of them sat down to talk for nearly an hour. Despite his rising fame, George was more interested in getting to know Gordy than focusing on his own story. He wanted to know about Gordy's experiences in Vietnam and how he started barefooting. George's secret to making friends all over the world was simple: be more interested in the other person's story than your own. There's a quote from the Dalai Lama that expresses this beautifully, "If you shift your focus from yourself to others, extend your concern to others, and cultivate the thought of caring for the well-being of others, then this will have the immediate effect of opening up your life and helping you to reach out."

George autographed a card featuring himself barefooting on one foot and holding the handle in his teeth. He signed it, "Banana 79 5/12." As he became older, George began signing all of his memorabilia with his age including the month, a wonderful reminder to everyone that time was indeed precious and to count every bit of it.

Gordy and George kept in touch, and a few weeks later, Gordy flew to Florida to spend a weekend at George's Winter Haven home. "I walked up to the front door and George's feet were imprinted into the concrete—in bright yellow," Gordy recalled.

The visit was the beginning of a close friendship. The two of them sat on the couch and talked for three-and-a-half hours. Just as at the airport, George was deeply interested in learning about Gordy's life rather than talking about his own. "I got to know George, the man, not Banana George, the showman," Gordy said.

Inventors of Thrills

Living in Florida, it didn't take George long to meet Bill Kitchen, his kindred spirit as an inventor and lover of an adrenaline rush. At the time, Bill was a well-known thrill ride inventor in Kissimmee, Florida. Bill introduced the Sky Coaster to George. You are strapped into a harness in a prone position, then hoisted to the top of a 300' tower and dropped, swinging like a pendulum. Bill also introduced George to his iSky, a wind tunnel. George put on a special flight suit and "flew." These are the kinds of activities the family had when visiting George and JoAnne in Florida, not your typical grandparent activities.

Footin' Behind a Seaplane 1996

Every year in Oshkosh, Wisconsin, pilots gather for the Experimental Aircraft Association convention. Nearby, for the 106th anniversary celebration of the town of DePere, Gordy Anderson put together a team of seven barefoot water skiers to ski individually behind a seaplane. It took several months to arrange for FAA clearance for the event. This was George's opportunity to make history as the oldest person to barefoot behind a plane.

When Gordy called the Blairs to tell them about the event, JoAnne was not happy. She knew all too well how cold the weather could be in Wisconsin on Memorial Day weekend. At 5:30 a.m. on the day of the event, she was right. Everyone bundled up in heavy coats and hats. The temperature registered cold and the wind 18 mph NE. Gordy took one look at the river and knew they were in for a rough day. There was no calm water to be found anywhere. They didn't have much choice—seven skiers were scheduled to barefoot behind the plane, the EAA (Experimental Aircraft Association) film crew was on site, and everything was in place.

"We're going to run a MasterCraft boat about 100 yards in front of you to smooth out the water," Gordy explained to George.

Gordy recommended stepping off a ski, but George was more comfortable doing his usual start by riding horizontal to the water, supine, with his feet wrapped around the ski line and head thrown back under water. He tried twice behind the plane, but he was unable to stand up and ski away.

As you know by now, tenacity is George's middle name and he wasn't about to give up. He tried once again; this time he got up on two skis, dropped a ski, and then kicked off the other ski.

He did it! George was barefooting behind a plane!

> But George wasn't content to do it just one time; he had to do it a second time. (Never waste a crowd, especially when it's on film.) After all, at eighty-one years and four months of age, there was no telling when he'd have another chance at making history behind an aircraft. Afterwards, an elated George climbed into the pick-up boat. The video aired on ESPN2 for a year. To view this video, visit his website: www.BananaGeorgeBlair.com

Later at the hotel, George and JoAnne were making plans for dinner when JoAnne spied a policeman walking up the path toward the lobby. Just then, the phone rang.

"They're after me," George said.

JoAnne thought he was joking. She picked up the phone. It was the hotel manager.

"There's a policeman here looking for Mr. Blair."

"All right, we'll be down," JoAnne said.

When George left the ski site, he had accidentally backed into a large statue of the many fish that make their home in Wisconsin, knocking it down like a stack of Legos and putting a dent in the rental car.

Oops!

Movie Star, *Captiva Island* 1995

"You're never too old to run down a dream, and never too young to catch one."

At a Cypress Gardens show, George met John Biffar, a fellow barefoot water skier. The two of them often joined World Barefoot Champion Ron Scarpa for barefoot runs together. John, a film director working for CBS at the time, was enthralled with George's energy and fervor. "I want to make a movie showing people how to live life to the fullest," he told George during one of their ski sessions.

John hired a scriptwriter, William Schreiber, to craft a story about a young, rich kid who goes on an adventure and meets three "mature-aged" guys who teach him a thing or two about life.

When the script for the new movie arrived on George's desk, he was beyond thrilled. The $1.7 million independent film, *Captiva Island*, fit him perfectly. The film also starred young Jesse Zeigler and Amy Bush, with old-timers Arte Johnson (*Laugh-In*), Ernest Borgnine, Bob Hite, and Bill Cobbs. The story centered on a sixteen-year-old who unexpectedly ends up on Captiva Island and encounters senior citizens who redefine what it means to be "old." George played himself, a "seventy-nine-year-young local who believes age is not a state of mind, but a state of exhilaration."

The movie required a teen who could barefoot water ski, and George immediately knew which kid he wanted to star in the movie with him: Johnathan Conner. John's father, Danny, was involved with barefoot competition and frequently volunteered at George's tournaments.

Neither George nor Johnathan had any acting experience, so they simply had to learn on the job. "Don't think about it; just do it!" George told Johnathan. The two of them practiced the barefooting scenes on dry land until they both knew every move by heart.

George loved every minute of being on the set and learning how to present himself for each scene. He handed out bananas to everyone. "We were pretty sick of bananas by the end," Director John Biffar said.

The film was shot on several locations in Florida, including Bonita Springs, Goodland, and Fort Myers Beach. When it came time to film the barefooting scene between George and Johnathan, the crew piled into George's yellow boat and headed out to find calm water.

"One thing I learned from watching George is that age is a state of mind," John, the director, said. "George taught me that if you don't use it, you lose it. He also proved that it's mind over matter—if you don't mind, it doesn't matter."

The film premiered on November 25, 1995 at the Reg Lenna Civic Center in Jamestown, New York. The Blairs hosted a second showing in Steamboat Springs, Colorado, to commemorate George's eighty-fifth birthday. The movie was shown on HBO, Showtime, and in theatres around the country. It also aired in Europe, Asia, Canada, South America, Africa, Australia, and New Zealand.

Eighty-Fifth Birthday Bash

The Chateau at Trails Edge was the fabulous private home that George rented in Steamboat Springs for his eighty-fifth birthday bash. It accommodated the whole family of sixteen people with six master bedrooms, a dorm room, game room, and hot tub, and it served as a ski-in and ski-out location. Each guest in the party wore a yellow ski bib that read: Banana George Blair's 85th Birthday Bash, Starring in *Captiva Island*. Everyone skied and snowboarded together as The Banana Team. Three of the grandsons bleached their hair yellow in honor of the yellow theme.

A gala birthday party bash was held at the Chateau followed by the premiere of *Captiva Island* at the local cinema. The director and some of the crew partied with George, his family, and many friends.

Eighty-Eighth Birthday 2003

For George's birthday friends and family gathered for a celebration dinner. His four daughters sang Cole Porter's "My Heart Belongs to Daddy," accompanied by Bernie Yaged playing the piano. An old friend Don Bonhaus penned this poem.

> *By George! There's a geezer named Blair,*
> *Whose moves are all made with a flair;*
> *Always ready to do*
> *Any challenge that's new,*
> *His next: who knows what, when or where?*

Chapter 16
Skiing for the King

In 1980 and 1984, George was invited to do an international water ski tour with the elite Cypress Gardens water ski team. The team performed in many countries, including Denmark, Sweden, and Norway. George was the oldest skier and the team accepted him as one of them.

"Every day after we did the show, we would be back on the road in the tour bus," said Lynn Novakofski, the show director. "George would break open a can of sardines, one of his favorite healthy snacks. However, the fishy odor was not appreciated by everyone."

During one tour, the team was invited to perform for King Hussein of Jordan, who was a water ski enthusiast, for his birthday celebration. He wanted the best American show skiers to be part of the royal festivities.

The weather was not optimal for performing—the wind was gusting.

"Be careful," the driver, Mark Voisard, warned George. "Don't fly the kite in bad wind."

But George did not want to disappoint King Hussein. He skied off with the flat kite. He ascended to perform his aerial tricks, but the strong gusts of wind were too much. He and the kite crashed into the water. George broke several ribs. When he climbed into the boat, the color was gone from his face. Fortunately, there was no internal bleeding and he healed quickly.

While the skiers were guests of the king they got the royal treatment, staying in the royal apartments. The team had a chance to shop. When George expressed his desire to return to New York with jewelry for his wife and daughters, King Hussein insisted that he shop only with the royal jeweler.

"When Dad returned from his trip, he and Joanne invited us to their apartment on Madison Avenue to celebrate. After a lovely dinner and Dad's stories about the king, the ski show, and shopping in Jordan, he brought out five stunning gold necklaces of different designs. We were very pleased to each choose the style we liked most," Robin recalls.

"Years later in April 2014, Dad was being honored posthumously with a Special Lifetime Tribute by the USA Water Ski Foundation at its Thirty-Second Annual Water Ski Hall of Fame Induction Ceremonies along with Cheryl Orloff. My sisters and I were wearing our gold necklaces. A few of the women skiers attending the gala mentioned to us in casual conversation that they recognized the necklaces. *How could they?* we thought. They told us that they were on that trip to Jordan with Dad, and relayed a part of the story Dad never told us. After buying the gold necklaces, Dad realized he would have to declare them to customs, so to save money and any aggravation, he asked five team members to wear the necklaces through customs. They regaled us with stories of their time in Jordan with Dad. It was such fun to hear this account. We all laughed. That was so Daddy. The story came full circle."

Turkey in 1998

In 1998, Turkey hosted world champions at the Water Ski Cup. Fifty-three skiers from ten countries competed in slalom, trick, and wakeboard. During his exhibition, George decided to do a barefoot start by leaping off a wall of rocks. "Some photographers came over and asked me if I was really going to do it. I told them if they promised to photograph me in slow motion, I would do it."

George climbed up the wall carefully and chose a spot that gave him little room for error. He stood on a shelf of rock so narrow and small that his toes hung over the edge. He looked down. A few large boulders jutted out of the water. He would have to generate enough momentum to leap beyond the rocks.

George was never one to waste an opportunity for a good show—and photographs to boot. He leapt off the wall with great force and landed in the water perfectly. He skied off with a big smile on his face.

Footin' on the Amazon (and Down in Rio, Too)

"This is a wild goose chase if I ever experienced one!"

George and JoAnne were sitting in the back of a taxi barreling down a dirt path. George had intended to barefoot water ski on the Amazon river, but now they were deep into the jungle—and perhaps the Portuguese-speaking driver totally misunderstood their request to find a water skiing oasis somewhere on the outskirts of Manaus, the capital city of the Brazilian state of Amazonas. Perhaps the interpreter had said the wrong words when they initially looked for a taxi that could transport them to a boat and driver on the river. As the taxi lurched over a high mound of dirt, JoAnne grabbed the back of the front seat.

The driver fired off a stream of Portuguese, accompanied by dramatic gestures intended to reassure them of his competence. JoAnne poured through her Portuguese phrase book, desperately trying to find the words to convey their request once again.

Just then, the trees separated and the trail ended at a wide landing area with docks and boats. The driver jumped out, grinning from ear to ear, and motioned to follow him. They noticed a young man bent over the motor of a ski boat.

"Hello! I am Joao Bartz, the night manager of the Tropical Hotel Manaus." He seemed quite delighted to meet George and JoAnne. He was excited at the idea of George water skiing barefoot behind his boat, and he reassured him that the engine would be fast enough. But first, they would have to take another bumpy ride to reach the edge of a sandy island on the Rio Negro (Black River.)

"I don't believe my eyes—look at those yachts!" George looked at the water, it was indeed black.

JoAnne shared her memories in an article she wrote in *The Water Skier Magazine*:

> After lunch, George donned his wetsuit. I did ask about the piranhas and Joao told us that everything would be all right as long as no one bled in the water! Everyone reinforced Joao's statement about piranhas attacking only when there is blood. However, I'm glad I hadn't as yet read the World Book's description of these deadly fish: "PIRANHA (Pih RAHN yuh) a bloodthirsty fish of

the Amazon River. Some scientists consider it more dangerous than a shark. Piranhas range from only about 4 to 18 inches long but attack in great numbers. Thousands of them sometimes travel in a group and they have been known to tear all the flesh off the skeleton of an animal or a human being in only a few minutes."

George gave several barefoot demonstrations, thus accomplishing his goal of footing on the Amazon. Everyone was thrilled and we spent the rest of the day on the island with our new friends.

George and JoAnne took off to the Guanabara Bay where George barefooted across the highly-polluted waters. After his first run, they went to Niteroi Bay, where the water was slightly less polluted and where George barefooted.

Next, they headed to Sao Paulo to visit friends for a couple of days. George immediately sought out and found a kindred soul with a boat on Lake Guarapiranga who would pull him for a few runs.

Their next stop was the capital city of Brasilia, smack dab in the middle of the country. "There's a man-made lake there, but it's impossible to find a way to barefoot in Brasilia," their travel agent warned them.

"That's what you think!" George chuckled. A local resident took them to meet Andre Assis, an avid skier who owned a 115-hp boat and had even tried barefooting himself. George barefooted through several runs, and JoAnne skied on a slalom ski. Then it was Andre's turn. Not only did George teach him to barefoot, but he also taught him to master the deep water start. Andre was a happy man when they left.

CHAPTER 17

Renaissance Man

GEORGE WAS A Renaissance man, a rare combination of education, business success, and athleticism, equally comfortable in a tuxedo and a wetsuit. There were so many layers to George, so many dimensions. When his grandsons—Robbie, Marcus, Ted, and Oliver—took up snowboarding, George was intrigued. On a trip to Crested Butte, Colorado, George decided to ditch the skis and learn how to snow board. His first ride on a snowboard was January 26, 1991, at age seventy-six.

George took it easy on the first couple of runs and quickly discovered that his water skiing experience translated perfectly to the snowboard.

On February 19 that same year, George returned to Crested Butte with Marcus. "I'm ready to hit the slopes!" George told his grandson on the second morning. Marcus rode up the chairlift with him and gave him instructions about how to dismount the chairlift on a snowboard. George hopped off the chairlift, and in his haste, the snowboard went one way and George went another. He tried to stand up, but the pain in his ankle was just too much.

The ski patrol arrived with a sled and whisked George to the base; then he transported him to the hospital. To George's great disappointment, the hospital x-rays showed a broken ankle.

The vast majority of people over the age of seventy might have called it a day and abandoned the sport at that point in their lives, but not George. That little taste of snowboarding was enough to ignite a new passion. He wanted more—and he was determined to master the sport. Once his ankle healed, George took to the slopes again. He found his niche at Steamboat Springs, where he met Billy Kidd, the director of the ski program there. The two of them skied together so much that they were often featured together in newspaper articles about Steamboat Springs. In the October 1995 issue of *Skiing* magazine, which encouraged the older crowd to take to the slopes, George, of course, got a mention.

Steamboat Springs, located on the west end of the Continental Divide, is known as a cowboy town. George bought himself a condo, and a cowboy hat that he promptly spray-painted yellow. In a short time, George became just as famous on the slopes as he was on the water. Skiers gathered around him at the base of the chairlifts and on the top of every run.

"Hey, Banana, can we get a picture with you?"

"George! I saw you on TV!"

"Hi, George. Can you autograph my board?"

"In searching for your purpose in life, remember, it should be something you enjoy doing and, it must give back to the world."

— Billy Kidd, Olympic Skier

Central Park

"My first grandson, Robbie, is the only person to water ski in Central Park in New York City," said George proudly. How did that happen? The Inflatable Boat Manufacturer Association contacted George, through the Family Ski School, about the association's convention in New York City. It wanted to demonstrate the versatility of inflatable boats and their recreational uses, especially to show a model that could be used as a ski boat. By special permission, an inflatable was allowed on the Central Park Lake for a demonstration. The horsepower was restricted, not enough for a barefooter, so Rob did a trick skiing run. There was a mayhem of boats shooting video for the media. They stole the show on the evening news.

Sebastian Eggert's Memories

Seb Eggert was George's sister Betty's son. Here he shares some of his personal memories of time he spent with Uncle George:

George was very masculine. He had a big personality. He was very passionate. If he was interested in something, he would go all out.

When I went to college, he helped me. He gave me an old truck to use, let me borrow it for the summer, then let me keep it. Later, he gave me a van from his insect business; it wasn't worth much to him, but it meant a lot to me. I couldn't afford to buy a car. My parents couldn't buy one for me.

Another time, he took me to Barneys New York Men's Store and bought me a suit. He said, "Seb, you need nice clothes. You are a good-looking young man. You need deodorant; you need to start shaving." He demanded that I grow up, instead of being a sloppy, dirty kid. He inspired me. I consider him my second father because he told me things I needed to know.

We did some business deals together. I needed money to expand my design and fabrication of fine architectural woodwork business. He would loan me money to buy equipment. I would pay him back with interest. He wrote an IOU that we both signed. I learned that it was important to have a formal agreement when doing business with family.

He talked to me about how to be a man, what my role is as a father and breadwinner. When I had some business debt, he said, "You must work every day, every single day, do some work every day, until you are out of this mess; promise me to do that. You have to be serious about your job." With that advice, I've never looked back. I'm very successful now; people recognize my quality work. He taught me: Work every day, don't be grumpy, be businesslike, do the job. I've always enjoyed my work, but by his example, he showed me a way to live my life. His gusto for life was amazing. Sometimes when I get up in the morning, I feel like, "Not again"… but then I tell myself, "Do It." It is a simple lesson. I learned that from him.

He always took care of his sister, Betty, my mother. He knew about her health problems and her limited funds, and he made sure to provide for her. She was always grateful for his generosity.

My brother, Kip, liked games like chess and backgammon. He played the stock market. He tried to convince George that a favorite stock would go over 1,000. George didn't agree. They had a $100 bet. When it went over 1,000, George paid him the $100.

When Donna and Bernie were married, they had a big vegetable garden, but in their woods, they grew marijuana. One holiday when we got together, Donna baked pot brownies. She called them "whole wheat" brownies. George, Betty, my dad, and all the cousins were stoned on the brownies. It was crazy, but we all had such a good time.

I remember there were unusual automatic toilets in his house. You had to be careful because you might be surprised; something weird could happen with the toilet!

Clean Machine

"Oh, Daddy, what is that?" said a curious ten-year-old GeeGee. She had discovered a strange fixture next to the toilet in their Havana, Cuba, hotel room. It was 1955, the first trip to a foreign country for Donna and GeeGee with their parents. The object in question, George answered, was a "bottom washer." This answer drew giggles from the two little girls at the age when anything peepee-poopy was fascinating. It was a bidet, a bathroom fixture common in Europe and other countries but little known in the United States.

George, being fastidious about personal hygiene, soon had a gadget afixed to the toilet at their home on Buttonwood Drive. The Mr. Bidet attached under the toilet seat, and when a lever was pushed, it sprayed a stream of warm water on your posterior. This was a brilliant way to make clean up more effective. It was especially useful for feminine hygiene, and there were five females in the house.

It became a curiosity for the neighborhood children. "We were happy to demonstrate how it worked by having our friends stand in front of the toilet, then pushing the handle, which sprayed a stream of clean water on the surprised observer," said GeeGee. "Of course, anything having to do with toilets was funny for children."

George was always searching for better bidet attachments. The bathroom at Buttonwood was too small for a traditional bidet, and he liked the efficiency of having it attached to the seat.

He experimented with any new versions that were invented. He even had a portable bidet for travel. It was a handheld, battery-operated, palm-sized pump with a retractable nozzle. You filled it with warm water, and then pushed a button to release a stream of water when it was positioned appropriately.

A Japanese company, Toto, created a complex toilet-bidet. When it became available in the United States, George became a dedicated customer. These toilets have heated seats with multiple warm water spray options, a warm air dryer, lids and seats that open and close automatically, an automatic flush, a vent to eliminate odors, and a night-light.

George bought each of his daughters one of these top-of-the-line Toto bidet toilets (Neorest) as a gift in 2005. Most people won't spend many thousands of dollars on a toilet, but he was passionate about cleanliness and wanted to share his beliefs. In true George fashion, he most likely negotiated a good deal.

If you ever visited George's Lake Florence home in Florida, you would find a different bidet toilet in each of six bathrooms. Not only that, but he believed that urinals were more sanitary, so he had those installed in several bathrooms.

George preferred terry cloth towels that were small, rather rough, and light. No heavy, luxurious bath towels for this practical man. He wanted to get dry quickly and efficiently. He had stacks of these inexpensive towels, all yellow, of course.

☾

Memories from Chip Hall, *Surfing* magazine

Chip Hall recalls how he first met George:

> Bill Biberbach of Ron Jon Surf Shop made a call to Craig Carroll of the Cocoa Beach Surfing School, and asked whether we thought it was possible to teach an octogenarian to surf. Carroll

was skeptical and immediately envisioned the typical Florida retiree: large car, oversized sunglasses, driving in the fast lane at 25 mph with a left turn signal constantly flashing. When Craig asked whether I could help with a lesson involving an eighty-three-year-old, I thought Dr. Kevorkian had devised an elaborately twisted suicide plan for this gentleman. After further researching Banana's abilities and taking into consideration his many accomplishments, we decided to give it a shot. Craig and I had the extreme pleasure of teaching Banana the fundamentals of this great sport. After briefing Banana on ocean safety and explaining how to get to his feet, we were ready to charge the three-foot shorebreak—and once in position, we set Banana up for his first ride.

Years of being towed by a boat had taken its toll on his shoulders. He was not able to do the traditional push up from the prone position, so we had to start him off on his knees. Hopping to his feet on his first try, Banana George had a style that would have made Duke [Kahanamoku, the father of modern surfing] himself nod in approval. By now, a good-sized crowd had gathered to see what all the fuss was about. Banana, never one to disappoint his fans, put on one heck of a show and even had the snowbirds hooting after each ride. Walking back out for one last wave, we asked Banana how it felt to get to his feet. He looked at us with that million-dollar smile and said, "Brother, let me tell you, it's the greatest feeling in the world!"

The Need for Speed

All his life, George had a heavy foot while driving and a fistful of speeding tickets to prove it. JoAnne surprised him with an enrollment in Skip Barber's racing school as a Christmas gift. George was excited—three whole days on a track racing as fast as he wanted to!

When he arrived at the track, it was no surprise that George was the oldest student there. It was hardly the first time he was involved in an activity with people less than half his age.

"I don't run from such situations; I revel in them," George said. "Another secret to my 'Do It' lifestyle is that I surround myself regularly with people, many who are young and have a desire to learn to do whatever it is we're gathered to do."

After three days of instruction, the final day culminated in a race. George had a blast roaring around the track.

In a subsequent visit to the Skip Barber headquarters in Lime Rock, Connecticut, George was scheduled for another race. When he arrived, he felt uneasy because it had begun to rain. By the time he reached the pit, the rain was coming down at a steady pace.

"We love to race in the rain," one of the regulars told him.

Fueled by the other drivers' enthusiasm, George pushed aside his apprehension and got into his car. The gun went off and all the cars lurched forward. By the second lap, the rain was pouring down. George could hardly see through the windshield. After the third lap, George pulled into the pit stop.

"I realized I didn't have the confidence to continue driving in those conditions," George said. "So much for my image as a daredevil!"

At that moment, there was a loud crash.

One of the drivers had slid into a stack of tires, but luckily, he emerged from his car with only broken wrists.

George commented, "I guess the message here is, when you don't feel confident in a situation, you can (and perhaps should) elect to *not* 'Do It.' There's no shame in that, and in some instances, it may save your life."

Robin recalls when George had a run-in with the police:

> There was an incident in Colorado. Dad had been at an all-day water ski tournament doing exhibitions, handing out his cards and bananas, and spreading his joy for life! But he was late in leaving the site to drive back to town to catch the TV show he was going to be on. He was rushing to get to the condo when he heard the all-too-familiar sound of the police siren.
>
> He pulled over and anxiously waited for the policeman to approach. The officer said, "Banana George, why were you going so fast?" Surprised, Dad said, "How do you know who I am?" The policeman explained, "I was at the tournament today and you gave me your card and a banana; besides, I recognized your yellow car." Dad replied, "Well, I'm trying to get back to town in

time to see myself on TV." The policeman said, "Okay, I know a bar close by with a TV—follow me!" With sirens blaring, Dad got a police escort to the nearest watering hole. He and the officer watched the news clip together of Dad bare footing and doing his signature trick, rope-in-teeth, to the applause of the crowd. Dad later commented, "Best banana I ever gave out!"

Monaco

One of George's favorite "race car" memories involved Prince Albert of Monaco. It began with a barefoot tournament in France, where George was scheduled to give exhibitions.

JoAnne shared her memories of meeting Prince Albert:

> We first met Prince Albert of Monaco at a water ski tournament in the south of France at Roquebrune-sur-Argens. Prince Albert was an avid water skier and a member of the Olympic Committee (which was considering adding water skiing as an event). He came to watch the tournament.
>
> Someone from Prince Albert's entourage came up to me and asked whether it might be possible for the prince's two young nephews to ride in the boat when George gave his exhibitions. I said I certainly thought it would be possible and I would tell George. Of course, George was delighted to honor the prince's request, and the two boys were very happy to ride in the boat and see barefooting up close.
>
> Shortly after we returned to Florida, an impressive-looking envelope arrived from the palace of Monaco. It was an invitation from Prince Albert to attend the Fifty-Eighth Monaco Automobile Grand Prix 2000. We were delighted to accept.
>
> We went to our Paris apartment for a few days, then left for Nice at the end of May 2000. We were greeted at the airport by a member of the palace staff and brought to the Hotel de Paris in Monaco.
>
> The big race took place on June 3. George was permitted to wear

his yellow suit and cowboy hat for this appearance—up until then he dressed conservatively.

George and I were at the starting gate with Prince Albert. The prince explained that George would be riding with him in his Ferrari through the race route. Just as the prince and George took off, someone said to me, "We're following," leading me into another Ferrari. We raced through Monaco with crowds of onlookers cheering from the sides. It was thrilling.

During the next couple of days, we were wined, dined, and enjoyed ourselves immensely. The festive and elaborate closing reception was on June 4 at the Monte-Carlo Sporting Club. Champagne flowed and the very chic crowd was in a celebratory mood.

"This week has truly been like a fairy tale to us," were George's parting words to Prince Albert.

Someone asked George, "Out of all the famous people you have mingled with over the years, who stands out the most and why?"

"Well, I'd have to say Prince Albert," he said. "He's down to earth. We were his guests for four days and four nights. I admire the way he lives his life. He is joyous and carefree, yet responsible. He's following in the footsteps of his father. He put me in his race car and we opened the ceremony of the weekend-long Grand Prix with 150,000 people watching! My wife and I were attended to by everybody. We felt like royalty! Prince Albert is a barefooter as well."

Footin' in China

George, JoAnne, and a fellow barefooter, Zenon Bilas, took off for China to perform in several exhibitions on a lake about thirty minutes from Beijing. The conditions on the first day were not favorable—the water was very cold and rough. During the first show, George opted to put on his regular wetsuit instead of a drysuit.

While George was in the boat, he grabbed a bottle of what he thought was water and took a swig. He immediately cringed.

"It tastes like soap," he said.

"It is soap!" the Chinese interpreter laughed. George had grabbed a bottle of dish soap used to make it easier to get a foot into the binding of a ski.

"When George went to ski, I could hear the engine sputtering—the boat was too slow for barefooting—maybe 30 mph," Zenon recalled. "Eighty-five-year-old George did a great job despite the slow speed. He got up and barefooted with spray in his face. He was a showman and determined to give everyone a show. We even took pictures in our barefoot wetsuits at the Great Wall of China."

Chapter 18
Bulls and Broken Backs

As supportive as JoAnne was with so many of his various endeavors, eighty-five-year-old George, who had long worn a cowboy hat, opted not to tell her about his next adventure: bull riding school.

But JoAnne found out anyway:

> I was in our kitchen in Florida. George was snowboarding in Steamboat and was due back home the next day. The phone rang. It was Robin. "Is Daddy really going to ride that bull?" she asked.
>
> "What bull?" Robin could hear the panic in my voice.
>
> Robin gave me the details. George was in Denver at a three-day bull riding school, taking lessons from World Champion Hall of Fame Bull Rider, Charles Sampson. He was scheduled to graduate that day with his first ride in the ring.
>
> As you might imagine, I had a couple of very bad hours before I heard back from George. He had gone through the training, riding a stationary bull, and passed with flying colors. Everything was set for him to go into the ring on the back of the bull. He was eighty-five years old and very determined to ride that bull. He was sitting in the starting gate on the back of the bull. The gate swung open, the bull lunged—and an instructor pulled George off the bull's back.
>
> George was infuriated—but unharmed. He was awarded a certificate for completing the school's curriculum but never got over not being permitted to finish!

Two Broken Backs—in One Year!

The 2001 Hot Foot Championships were held on Lake McCormick in Seffner, Florida. The wind was high that day, coming off a recent storm, and the water was not smooth. At eighty-six, George was still pushing the boundaries as a competitor. He was officially the world's oldest competitive barefoot water skier. He completed his slalom event and put a score of 3.0 on the board.

The next day, George stood on the dock preparing for his trick run. "Hey, brother!" He tossed his handle to the boat crew. A crowd gathered around the shore to watch George get ready for his usual Flying Dock start.

This time, George misjudged his leap, slipped, and landed with his back on the dock. He bounced off and landed in the water upside down, unable to move. In an instant, the other skiers dove in and carefully righted him so he could breathe. Char Portman, the tournament safety director, ran to get the back board.

The pain was excruciating for George. As he was whisked off to the hospital, a somber mood settled over the competitors at the tournament. They feared it would be the last time George ever barefoot water skied.

An x-ray showed a cracked vertebra. It was the third time George had fractured a vertebra in his back.

"We heard he broke his back, and we had a horrible time getting through the rest of the tournament," Danny Conner said. "When we went to visit him in the hospital, he was in good spirits and felt he would heal up completely. He could move his toes and legs. We were blessed that he healed and barefooted again. He let others know that you're never too old." Two other competitors also suffered minor injuries that day.

After several months, George felt healed enough to get back on the water again. He did some light skiing with the boom to get his strength back. George did two runs on the boom and then added a rope for his third run. He even managed to barefoot on one foot twice. "I feel great! I'm so happy to be doing this," he said.

In November that same year, George was out practicing his trick run behind the boat and took a fall. As soon as he hit the water, the same familiar pain came flooding back. "I hurt so much I felt like I was going to die," George told a reporter from *The Ledger*. The x-ray showed a compression fracture on another vertebra. This time, George made sure he took a little more time to heal before he was back out on the water again.

"His perennial optimism and ability to laugh away any setbacks were the source of his success," Carrie said.

The Surgeon Who Became George's Neighbor

During one of George's practice runs, he was working on landing a jump out of two skis, something he had done successfully many times before—only this time, his foot caught on the water and snapped forward. He tore his ACL. George met up with Dr. Stephen Beissinger, an orthopedic surgeon in Florida who offered surgery or rehabilitation.

"I've got to get back on the water in six weeks," he told the doctor.

"No way," Dr. Beissinger said. "It can take up to one year after surgery to rehabilitate to a normal activity level."

But George was stubborn. George opted out of surgery and did physical therapy. He was set to do a filming for *The Guinness Book of World Records*—it was arranged months before. Six weeks later, Dr. Beissinger stood on the shore and watched as George barefooted by him with a big smile on his face, a "thumbs up"—and his knee in a brace.

When the property next to the Blairs came up for sale, the Beissingers purchased the stately home and moved in. They were soon part of the "extended" family; Stephen, his wife Chris, and their children Ryan and Megan.

"One of the life lessons I learned from George was to never give up, and never give in," Chris recalled. "Always set the bar high and be forever young. George encouraged people to follow their passion. He had a zeal for life—and it was contagious!"

CHAPTER 19
Media Star

In his eighties, George was more popular than ever. His phone rang constantly with requests for interviews, media appearances, and speaking gigs. Stock photo agencies used his images for billboards, magazines, book covers, and greeting cards. He was recognized all over the world.

George received a postcard in August 2000 written by his friend:

> A couple of years ago I found you skiing across my TV screen in South Africa, remember? Now, I am driving up the road out of Dubrovnik (Croatia) and Wow!! There is a roadside billboard featuring The Banana Man, yellow wetsuit and all. Incredible! I didn't see the product name and didn't get a chance for a second look. Nice going.
>
> Don Bonhaus

Ads/Endorsements/Sponsors

Sponsors clamored to have George use their products: Intensity (wetsuits), Body Glove (wetsuits), Bollé (sunglasses), Nitro (snowboards), Clicker (bindings), Clincher (gloves), US Gear (ski handles). He appeared in print and television ads for Armor All. Anywhere in the world when opening a newspaper or magazine, one might find him skiing across the page in *Barrons*, the *Wall Street Journal, Men's Journal, Advertising Age, AARP Magazine, The National Enquirer, Family Circle, Prevention, Reader's Digest, Modern Maturity, Télé 7 Jours, Florida De-*

partment of Elder Affairs, and *Delta Upsilon Quarterly*. His iconic barefooting picture was used in ads for various health products, insurance companies, vacation packages, dental practices, medical centers, money management companies, and calendars. It is impossible to list all the publications in which he was featured as an inspiration.

When *Sports Illustrated for Women* put George in the magazine, they completely redefined what it means to be sexy in the later years. George was clad in a yellow bikini-style swimsuit and flanked by two women in yellow bikinis. In January 2003, he told a reporter for the *St. Petersburg Times*: "I never thought of myself as one of the world's sexiest men, but I like it."

Of course, there were often articles in the *Water Ski, Water Skier, Ski Nautique,* and *Wasser Ski* magazines about him, and he appeared on their covers many times.

Live with Regis and Kathie Lee

George appeared on the morning TV talk show *Live with Regis and Kathie Lee* twice. On the first show, George made his entrance being pulled on water skis. When he hopped out of the skis, as instructed by the TV crew, Kathie Lee was surprised and lost her balance, stumbling backwards. George ran over and caught her.

"They told me you were beautiful, but I had no idea you were dynamite too!" George told her.

The second appearance was filmed in Hawaii and featured George barefooting in the bay. He loved the attention that Regis and Kathy showered on him.

The Late Show with David Letterman

When George was scheduled for *The Late Show with David Letterman*, friends warned him to be prepared to be roasted on the show. George paid no attention to the warnings and walked into the show with confidence. From the start, Dave seemed enthralled with George.

DL: So, George, how old are you?

GB: I'm seventy-seven.

DL: You look like a man of fifty.

GB: You say I look fifty, but when I look in the mirror, I feel eighty-two!

DL: You are goofy! I mean that with all due respect. Tell me about the skiing accident you had a few years ago.

GB: Five years ago, I was practicing barefoot jumping at my Lake Florence house. The first jump was my personal best. A beautiful jump, forty feet! I went for a second jump and, David, I was so euphoric I wasn't concentrating. I looked up. When I hit that ramp, my knees buckled, the base of my spine hit that ramp at forty miles an hour, and I flew off into the air and I thought…my rump hit the ramp! God, I think I broke my back. I think I'm going to die.

DL: But you survived! And that might be one of those sentences that no other man has ever uttered: "*My rump hit the ramp!*"

The Oprah Winfrey Show

Then there was *The Oprah Winfrey Show*. JoAnne was in Pittsburgh with her brother and his wife when George called. "You'll have to get on the next plane," he told her. "*The Oprah Winfrey Show* wants me in Chicago tomorrow."

When JoAnne arrived at the hotel, she could see George was in pain. "What happened?"

"I took a fall yesterday while barefooting and broke two ribs."

George was in so much pain that he had to sit up all night in a chair and couldn't sleep. It hurt just to breathe. When they arrived at Harpo Studios, George put on a game face as best he could, but it wasn't one of his best interviews. He couldn't be his usual, jovial self. When it came time to take a picture with Oprah, George broke into a smile. They hugged and he showed no trace of being in pain.

A Busy Schedule

When George was seventy-six, in 1991, he wrote a list of his activities for the previous twelve months.

1. Cypress Gardens sponsored my appearance at the eight stops in the United States of the Michelob Dry Professional Water Ski Tour. At each venue, I did a barefoot exhibition on Saturday as well as Sunday. At nearly every stop, the tour's promotional people asked me to do interviews and on-the-water demonstrations for the local newspapers, magazines, radio stations, and television.

2. The Cypress Gardens Advertising and Promotional Departments took me on a Canadian tour in Toronto, Ottawa, and Montreal, where I did interviews with media and did a number of on-the-water demonstrations.
3. Cypress Gardens included me with thirteen other skiers on a team that went to French Guiana, South America for one week during the World Cup Tournament. We did an average of four shows per day.
4. At the Grand Opening of the Overhead Cable Skiway, a new man-made water park in Phoenix, Arizona, I put on a barefoot demonstration.
5. At the National Barefoot Tournament in DuQuoine, Illinois, I took first place in jumping, second in tricks, third in slalom, and third overall in the over-fifty-five division.
6. The Chiquita Banana Company volunteered to set up a sponsorship with me and I said to them, "Do you know how long I have been waiting for this call?"
7. I appeared in a full-page ad for Cheerios in the November issue of *Prevention* magazine and *Reader's Digest*, as well as the December and March issues of *Modern Maturity*. Total circulation of these magazines is roughly 50 million copies, with roughly 125 million readers.
8. I authored the feature article in the March issue of *Water Ski* magazine, "Wild Dogs on the Parker Strip—Barefooting's Top Banana Reveals a Water Skier's Paradise."
9. I hosted the third annual Blairfoot Bananza—a barefooting endurance and mania contest taking place at Cypress Gardens.
10. I learned the sport of snowboarding, but managed to break my ankle getting off a lift.
11. I was elected to the Water Ski Hall of Fame.

The Show that Turned into a Wedding

Phil Keoghan, host of the *Amazing Race*, was working on a show in the 1990s called "Breakfast Time." The show featured ordinary people with fascinating stories. Phil's producer discovered George and booked him for the show.

"I didn't know anything about Banana George," Phil recalled.

When Phil and the crew arrived at George's house in Florida, he was greeted at the door by George, dressed in bright yellow and in bare feet. Phil was taken aback by George's energy. He showed the crew around the house, bounding up the stairs like a twenty-two-year-old and stopping in the living room to entertain them with an impromptu concert on the drums.

"He introduced us to his wife JoAnne—she was younger [by eighteen years]—he needed a young woman to be able to keep up with him!"

George's message on the show was simple: You can change in midlife—it's all in the mind.

Phil and George remained in contact after the show and became close friends. Phil continued to shoot George's story for other shows. Even after spending the entire day on a shoot, George would still have energy to dance at night while the rest of the crew was relaxing with cold beers. "He was a kid in an old body," Phil said. "Because of his positive energy, he did extraordinary things."

During one visit in Florida, the topic of barefooting came up.

"How come you don't barefoot?" George asked Phil.

"I've never tried," Phil explained.

"Come on; let's go. I will teach you. It will take us about an hour."

Just like that, they headed down to the boathouse and George geared up the boat. Phil had never barefooted before.

"Now remember," George said, "when you kick off the ski, don't look down."

No sooner did Phil kick off the ski than he looked down. He slammed into the water and popped to the surface, grimacing in pain.

"Don't give up. Come on; let's go again."

Phil didn't want to disappoint George, but he was already hurting. Less than an hour later, he was skimming along the water with a big smile on his face. George was beaming, too.

When it came time to celebrate his fifth wedding anniversary, Phil and his wife decided to renew their vows, underwater, and Phil asked

George to be his best man. George had an ear infection so he couldn't go underwater, but at a perfectly-timed moment during the ceremony, he dropped the wedding rings into the water.

"A lot of times I hear 'I'm too old for this or that'—people use age to determine what options are available," Phil said. "It's as if a number correlates with what life offers—but George never saw age as a restricting number. He was proud of talking about his age. I remember he signed a photograph for a cameraman and he signed it 83 and ¾."

George was part of the inspiration behind Phil's book, *No Opportunity Wasted*. Phil learned some wonderful life lessons from George, and he shares them with others when he travels internationally because he wants to inspire others to grab every bit of life. "It's important to focus on what you have and what you can do, as opposed to what you don't have and what you can't do," Phil explained. "George helped me understand that because he could have easily said, 'I'm too old; I don't have the strength'—instead, he used the body he had and the determination he had to do extraordinary things."

When George experienced pain in his shoulders and had trouble lifting his arms, he simply adjusted his movements and adapted to the limitations. He didn't see his limitations as a negative thing—he simply saw them as challenges.

"If there's one message that people can take from George, it is this: age does not determine what you can do in life. Age is simply a number, and that number does not have anything to do with the choices you make in life.

"George looked for and found the good in everyone. He taught me to find what is right in people instead of finding the wrong. He met people knowing that everyone has something to love about them—he focused on the positive—that's why so many people connected with him."

"The key to success is focus," George told a reporter for the *Delta Upsilon Quarterly*. "Everybody has to decide what they want to do. I don't care if it's a long-range plan, or a short-range plan, or whether the plans change. You have to have a focus."

Chapter 20

Ninety Years Young

On January 22, 2005, George turned ninety. This would be no ordinary day for this extraordinary man. The celebration started at the Cypress Gardens noon show. George shimmied into his customary yellow wetsuit. You couldn't miss the smile on his face—George was happy. Ninety years old felt pretty good! It was a special day on the water for George.

The whole family was gathered, dressed in yellow, in the front rows of the grandstand. When George finished his barefoot routine, the announcer, Alex Jacobson, roused the audience in singing "Happy Birthday," as two lovely Aqua Maids presented him with a splendid birthday cake decorated with bananas. The crowd erupted in cheers.

Lynn Novakofski said, "I was working on a photo montage for his ninetieth birthday. I watched a bunch of videos when he was on several talk shows: *Oprah*, *Good Morning America*, and others, which had been about fifteen years before his ninetieth. It was funny to me that they were talking about this remarkable old guy, at age seventy-five, who was still barefoot water skiing. How amazing, I thought, that Banana George was still doing it, at about the same skill level, fifteen years later at age ninety!"

On the evening of his birthday, fifty special friends and family gathered for a dinner party at George and JoAnne's Winter Haven home.

Carrie stood up to give a toast:

> I am Carrie Blair, third daughter of George and Dorothy Blair. For my ninetieth birthday, in 2038 to be exact, I'll be happy if a

few friends roll up their wheelchairs to help me blow out all the candles and gum a little birthday cake.

I wonder whether Daddy ever imagined he'd reach this milestone and what his idea of a proper celebration would be.

But just look around you at all the friends, fans, and family, his real wealth, he has wisely acquired in a flamboyant life working and playing hard, traveling the wide world, and sharing his enthusiasm and unique banana yellow charisma with anyone who will watch.

For the man who lives his whole life like a game of *Beat the Clock*, he's been rewarded with a long and healthy lifespan, outliving his parents' ages by decades.

In fact, he enjoys measuring the distance, time elapsed, miles per hour, weight, and money earned for nearly every aspect of his life, keeping meticulous charts and using a stopwatch.

I remember winning praise for climbing a rope in a backyard tree faster and faster while he urged me to try a little harder or longer.

He asks for, no, he demands your best, and you were so proud when you gave it, when you surpassed yourself, broke your own record, and exceeded expectations.

It is hard to exceed Daddy's expectations, but his praise was worth stretching for. He celebrated your accomplishment and reinforced his confidence that you could do it, that you were special, above average, even exceptional.

He was delirious with achievement and wanted more all the time. Every success was just a step to greater challenge, and as soon as one level was achieved, you had to go on to the next level.

Never be satisfied.

Why George gets out of bed every morning is the drive to try, again and again, to achieve what he accomplished yesterday, and maybe go beyond. What he wants is the challenge. Like every boy, he longs to be tested, to be found able, or exceptional.

Banana George needs to "foot" like most of us need to eat—it is an unavoidable necessity of his life. He thrives because of it. What most ninety-year-olds would find impossible he finds exhilarating, going out on the water for his daily dose of adrenaline and endorphins, seeking new thrills every day, and engines with a lot of "kick."

He shows relentless tenacity in achieving his goals, while calculating risks and benefits in every endeavor.

There is absolutely no way to exaggerate about Daddy. He broke new ground whatever he tried. Daring! Dazzling! Ambitious! Innovative!

He has a desire to excel and is an awe-inspiring over-achiever. Daddy's infectious good humor radiates out to all his well-loved crowds.

He is generous to a fault, sharing his time, talent, and wealth with scores of others.

He is a hero to young and old all over the world, and even at ninety, keeps his lifelong advice: "A quitter never wins; a winner never quits."

I am proud to swim in your gene pool. Happy birthday, Banana George.

Love, Carrie

Honorary Mayor of Cypress Gardens

On January 22, 2006, George turned ninety-one. He was honored for his decades of entertainment at the park by being named the Honorary Mayor of Cypress Gardens. He was even given a special parking space for his yellow Lincoln. All of the audience members wore yellow and gave George a standing ovation. Ron Scarpa and Lynn Novakofski gave speeches celebrating George's accomplishments. Lynn was the show director at Cypress Gardens and photographed George more than any other photographer.

"George is a big part of Cypress Gardens' history, and we needed to do something to recognize his time in entertaining people here," said Lynn Wright, the public relations manager for Cypress Gardens.

Snowboarding Fall

In February of 2006, Gordy Anderson, Oliver Fetter (George's youngest grandson), and George took off for Steamboat Springs to spend a few days on the slopes. On the morning of the first day, George decided to take it easy and stay off the slopes. "The altitude (6,732') might have affected him. After all, he was ninety-one-years-old," Oliver recalled. Nineteen-year-old Oliver took off for the chairlift and spent the day snowboarding on his own.

The next day, George woke up feeling great. The sun gleamed on the mountainside. The three of them headed to Wally's World, one of George's favorite spots on the backside of the mountain. Halfway down the Tomahawk run, George and Oliver paused for a snapshot from the resort photographer—both of them raising their arms and grinning from ear-to-ear. It was a special time for Oliver because it was the first time he had his grandfather all to himself without his cousins around.

After the photograph, the three of them took off again. George was carving his way at a fairly quick pace down the mile-and-a-half long run.

"Gordy, I can still ride!" George hollered. He burst into tears. Gordy understood. Despite the challenges of a body that was continually trying to slow him down, George could still push the limits of what he could do. He was enjoying every minute of being on the mountain in the crisp Colorado air.

They skied their way down to Thunderhead Lodge and met up with Oliver to take a break. "In typical Banana fashion, George was shaking hands with everyone and passing out cards," Gordy recalled.

After lunch, they rode the lift to the top again. This time, they took a different trail that was much more challenging. Oliver took off first.

"This run looks a little too narrow and steep," Gordy said.

"Oh, hey, brother, we'll be fine!" George insisted.

Gordy helped George onto his snowboard. He turned around to snap on his skis, put on his gloves, and follow him down.

A few seconds later, he heard an urgent yell.

"Gordy, Banana fell!"

Gordy took off like a madman and skied down to George. He was lying on his back with his head pointed downhill. He had caught an edge and went tumbling forward.

"Hey, brother, are you all right?"

George appeared dazed. "Who are you? What happened?"

Gordy's heart sank. George was clearly confused. Gordy took off his skis and stuck them in the snow behind George, making an "X" to alert the skiers and ski patrol that help was needed. The ski patrol arrived quickly. They wrapped a neck brace around George, bundled him, and strapped him in a rescue sled. When they reached the bottom, an ambulance was waiting. Oliver rode in the ambulance, and they headed to Yampa Valley Medical Center.

Shortly after, Gordy was relieved when he walked into the Emergency Room, "Hey, Gordy," George said.

It was a good sign that George recognized him and remembered his name. George was on a gurney, waiting for a doctor to arrive. A series of tests showed a mild concussion but no serious damage.

"You'll be released soon, but no more snowboarding for seventy-two hours," the doctor said.

A nurse came in. "I've gotta take your temperature and make sure it's normal before you leave." She asked George to sit up. He complied.

"I'm sitting on my $%#@ nuts!" he grumbled.

Oliver and Gordy looked at each other with glee.

"He's back!"

World Barefoot Tournament 2006

At the age of ninety, George was on top of the world, but after the snowboarding fall, his memory began to decline slowly. The cartilage in his shoulders was gone. He had been considering surgery for his "frozen" shoulder. It was difficult for George to raise his arms. That year, the

World Barefoot Tournament was held in Adna, Washington, and George was invited to attend. JoAnne stayed in Florida to organize the annual Blairfoot Bananza tournament, so Carrie attended the tournament with George. As soon as they walked into the lobby, George was flooded with photo and autograph requests. To greet the participants, the committee erected a flag pavilion at the entrance to the ski site, which George funded. After dinner, George stayed out late to catch up with old and new friends.

The next day, George was scheduled to barefoot during a break in the competition. There was a record-setting number of spectators and competitors. What the crowd didn't know was that for the first time in his life, George wasn't sure he could pull off the barefooting. The boat driver provided reassurance as George was about to begin. "Don't worry, George; we'll take care of you." The conditions were formidable—the cold wind produced a choppy surface and a spitting rain.

George took off on the boom and skied with a smile on his face. On the next pass, he managed a wave and to ski on one foot. The crew lifted him out of the water to thunderous applause. No one in the crowd realized how tough it was for George to accomplish his barefooting run. On the shore, he gave a short, cheerful speech, praising the sport and the wonderful people there.

"He made everyone cry," William Farrell recalled. "George himself was crying. That was his last big exhibition at a tournament."

"He was probably close to one of the last times he could barefoot," Carrie said. "He was so excited and grateful that he was still able to do it. He pushed himself to the edge. He almost didn't have the energy and strength to do it, but still, he went out there and did it."

CHAPTER 21

Unstoppable

In 2007, just before Christmas, George caught pneumonia while he and JoAnne were living in their New York apartment. JoAnne had never seen George so ill. He was having difficulty breathing, so she called 911. Twenty-four hours after George was admitted to the hospital, the doctors were not sure he would live through the night. JoAnne prepared herself for the worst and the whole family gathered.

But George remained just as tenacious as ever, refusing to give up on living just yet. After seven days in the hospital while his two daughters who were RNs managed his care, he was able to return home. But there would be no skiing for George on his ninety-third birthday. Instead, he spent the day being attended by his family and his home health aides, and waiting for a physical therapist to arrive.

After months of rehabilitation, George returned to Winter Haven. During an interview with a *Ledger* reporter, George said, "It'll kill me to sit on the sidelines, but it's what I have to do. It isn't easy being ninety-three."

George pulled up his pant leg and showed the reporter numerous barefooting bruises. "At forty miles per hour, something has to give. I've been too busy to properly treat these bruises."

There were tears in his eyes.

"I think I have to give up barefooting. When I get on the water, I go wild to see how far I can push an old body. I think it's tired of me pushing."

By all outward appearances, family and friends figured that it was time for George to truly stay off the water, but the crew at the TV show

Growing Bolder had other ideas. In March of 2008, Marc Middleton, the CEO, asked George whether they could film him barefooting once more.

George said yes.

JoAnne was worried. George was increasingly frail and had great trouble walking. How in the world would he be able to barefoot?

But George, stubborn, determined, passionate, wanted to get back on the water. JoAnne knew she could not stop him, but she would do everything she could to make sure he was as safe as possible.

When Marc and the crew from *Growing Bolder* arrived, they had no idea how compromised George really was. George was getting over a battle with pneumonia. It took two people to support him and ten minutes to walk from the house down to the boat. George was quiet—he was not his usual bubbly self. Marc thought George looked a little nervous about the whole thing.

"Should we stop him?" Marc asked JoAnne.

"Are you kidding? I can't stop him. Nobody can stop him."

JoAnne admitted she was worried, yet she knew George needed to do what he most loved.

George's driver, Lane Bowers, a champion barefoot water skier, evaluated the situation and decided to have George sit in the handle attached to the boom. This would provide him much-needed support during the actual barefooting. Gordy helped George into the swing and placed his hands on the boom. Lane backed the boat out.

Lane slowly accelerated and George put his feet on the water. He was a bit unsteady, but for a few seconds, he was barefoot water skiing.

George was setting another record—no other human to date could barefoot water ski at ninety-three years of age.

But George wasn't one to waste a crowd. If he was going to set a record, he was going to go *all out*. For one second, it looked like he picked up his right foot and skied on one foot. Barefoot water skiing on one foot—it was likely no other ninety-three-year-old could top that!

In a split second, George's feet came off the water and he began to twist sideways. When he let go of the boom, he swung around and fell head first and backwards into the water with a hard splash. It was the barefooter Roger, The Moose, who dove into the water and rushed out to George.

"Are you okay?"

George gave a "thumbs up" sign. "I'm positive!" he said.

In an earlier interview with *Growing Bolder*, George had said, "All of life is up and down. I don't wait for the next thing. I make the next thing happen."

Use It or Lose It

In June of 2008, George called Gordy and told him to get the boat ready. It was a beautiful sunny day and he wanted to go for a barefoot run off the boom. Another friend and fellow barefooter, Andy Lundt, came along.

"One thing I learned from George is to take advantage of the time you have, follow your passion, and don't let age define you," Andy said. "George had a 'use it or lose it' mentality. He wanted to live a long, fulfilling life—and he certainly did that. I remembered that George had an excellent way of coaching. Once, when I wasn't paying attention, he yelled, 'Why aren't you smiling? You are supposed to enjoy this. Take another run and this time smile.'"

Andy admired George's constant tenacity to improve his form and technique on the water. As he watched George gliding on the water, he snapped several pictures. He had no idea that this would be the last time George would ever barefoot water ski.

A few seconds later, George caught a toe and tumbled into the water. It was a pretty hard slam. Gordy whipped the boat around quickly and throttled the engine. George winced in pain.

"Are you okay, brother?"

George nodded. The guys helped him in the boat. "I'm done for the day," George said. "Take me back to shore and drop me off."

George was quiet on the way back to the dock. "We dropped him off; we thought he was just a little shook up—no big deal," Andy recalled.

A few days later, the guys learned what had really happened: George had broken a couple of ribs in that fall. He knew he was seriously hurt, but being the ever-tough showman, he didn't want to ruin a perfectly good skiing day for the other guys.

Breaking Records—Not Backs!

It took a few weeks for George's ribs to heal and for the pain to diminish. George realized that he was in no shape to continue to barefoot, but he could certainly enjoy the water on a pair of skis. One afternoon, Keith St. Onge, a World Barefoot Champion, came over to ski with George. Gordy drove the boat while the two of them skied side-by-side.

As time rolled on, George was having more difficulty walking and speaking due to the effects of Lewy body dementia. This condition is caused by abnormal collections of protein within the cytoplasm of neurons (known as Lewy bodies) and a loss of dopamine-producing neurons. It is classified as a neurodegenerative disorder. It is the same condition from which Kathie Lee Gifford's father, Robin Williams, and Dina Merrill suffered. Living in New York made it easier for him to get around, but JoAnne knew he missed the Florida sunshine and being on the water.

One day, JoAnne called Gordy. "Is there any way we can get him out skiing?" she asked. "I can't just take him to Winter Haven and let him look at the lake and not let him get on the water."

"JoAnne, he's just too frail," Gordy said gently. He knew there was no way George could safely stand up on skis at that point.

One afternoon, the phone rang. "JoAnne, I have an idea," Gordy said. "I'm involved with the adaptive skiing program in Florida with Ann O'Brine Satterfield. She uses a wheelchair and she teaches others how to ski adaptively. We can get George back on the water with a sit ski. It won't be barefooting—but he will be the oldest man in the world to do this. The previous record was held by a seventy-nine-year-old."

The event was arranged for June 19, 2009 on Lake Florence. "We're going skiing today!" Gordy explained. George's ability to communicate was minimal, but his eyes lit up when Gordy pulled on his wetsuit. To commemorate the occasion, they brought in a bright yellow sit ski and decorated the seat with yellow duct tape.

As Gordy, JoAnne, and Merlene (George's caregiver) walked him down to the dock, a dozen skiers shouted encouragement.

"Go, brother! You've got this, Banana! Have fun skiing!"

A team of skiers gently lifted George and lowered him onto the sit ski. Gordy and another volunteer slid his feet into the water skis and held George steady in the water. "In gear!" Gordy instructed the driver, Danny Connor. The rope slowly uncoiled and tightened.

"Hit it!"

The three skiers rose together and glided on the water. At ninety-four and five months, George was setting yet another record. When they arrived back on shore, George had tears streaming down his cheeks.

And as you know by now, George has to do things not once, but definitely twice. Ten days later, George went for another ski; this time he was flanked by two gals, Barb Muren and Ashley Townsend. Lynn Novakofski, the USA Water Ski photographer, captured a beautiful moment of both girls giving George a kiss on each cheek in mid-ski.

Yes, there was a huge smile on George's face.

"After that exhilarating ski, we returned to New York where all the doormen in our building gave George a big welcome and a 'high five,'" JoAnne said. "We decided to stay in New York, where George was very comfortable and there were many friends, family, and activities for him to enjoy. We had wonderful caregivers who were like family. We regularly went to jazz concerts and George had his drums to play. I rented an apartment a block away so that George could go "out for lunch" if he tired of his home surroundings or wanted to entertain in a different place. It also served as guest accommodations for many visitors coming to spend time with George."

Humans of New York

In 2010, Brandon Stanton, a photographer in New York, began a project of taking photographs of interesting people while walking the streets of Manhattan. Brandon posted the photographs on his Facebook page and included short stories of everyone he met. Here's an excerpt of what Brandon posted about George:

> I stumbled upon a National Treasure yesterday.
>
> I was walking down 3rd Avenue when I noticed an old man in a wheelchair. He was being pushed by an aide. Despite his frail condition, he had dressed with extreme care. He wore an out-

landish yellow outfit. Everything about him was yellow, from his shades to his socks. Intrigued by his appearance, I bent down and asked for a photograph. He silently nodded approval. After I'd taken his photograph, his aide offered a formal introduction: "This is Banana George," she said, "the world's oldest barefoot water skier. He's ninety-seven now. When he was ninety-two, he set the world record for the oldest person to barefoot waterski."

Banana George didn't even begin waterskiing until he was forty. But it soon became his passion. So much so that he began doing ski shows at Cypress Gardens. In the course of his career, he sustained a multitude of injuries. I've seen footage of a very old George being pulled through the water in a sit ski, smiling like a madman.

Banana George is a testament to loving life, and he deserves to be celebrated.

Even though George could not verbalize his story to Brandon, being a true showman, he still managed to have his story shared. After the *Humans of New York* post, George's Facebook page grew to over 127,000 fans. He was also featured in the *Humans of New York* book. To view a short video of Banana George skiing on his ninetieth birthday, visit his website: www.BananaGeorgeBlair.com

"I never sat around and thought about becoming famous," George said in an interview when he was eighty-eight. "I've been living my life the way I want to live it. You call it famous, some people call it celebrity—it wasn't planned that way, but I'm glad it's that way. I've always had a do-gooder attitude, that I wanted to make the world a better place. So many people say I'm their role model. It's very pleasing to know that I've done something to inspire people to do better for themselves and for the world."

George's great-granddaughter, Jessica Blair, said, "My great-grandfather taught me to live with love instead of fear; to me that is art. You are never too old to try new things and to encourage others to test their limits."

Chapter 22

All Good Things Come to an End

Grandson Ted often came from Vermont to visit George and Jo-Anne at their New York City apartment. He was familiar with the deteriorating condition of his grandfather and it pained him. In the autumn of 2013 when he came to visit, he entered the bedroom with trepidation, where he found GB in bed, staring into space.

With an upbeat voice, Ted greeted GB. As he sat next to him, Ted thought of happier days, when his grandfather would give him a big greeting and a hearty laugh. Ted knew he would have to carry on a one-sided conversation.

He wanted to share with GB some reminiscences: about jumping off the boat house roof into the lake, skiing, playing fierce games of ping pong and *Space Invaders*. He talked about what he was doing now, his music, politics, and current events. Nothing he said got a response. Ted felt so sad and conflicted. The Lewy body dementia GB had been diagnosed with had robbed his grandfather of his vital personality. Ted struggled with seeing his grandfather fading. He knew GB didn't want to be like this.

George had said many times, as the number of candles increased on his birthday cakes, "I want to die on the water, doing what I love to do—barefooting." Instead, George had become a prisoner in his own body.

One particular day, Ted thought of one last thing to share with his grandfather. He said, "You won't believe this, but in your honor, I planted a hardy banana tree. I did some research and found one that could grow in my Vermont greenhouse. The next time I see you, I hope to bring you a banana from my tree."

Ted was amazed at the immediate response. His grandfather looked up with tears welling in his eyes. GB said, "Awwwww, brother!"

"He saved that for me," Ted recalls. "It was classic GB! For a moment, he connected with me and the next moment he was 'gone,' just a blank stare. It was fleeting but it was beautiful—more than I could have hoped for.

"I felt that it was essentially our goodbye, my last chance to connect with my grandfather who had been larger-than-life to me."

Friend to Everyone

In an interview late in his life, George was asked, "What would you like to be remembered for the most?"

With a long, emotional pause, George said, "I wish the world would think of me as a man who loves his family and friends, and loves people. I wish the world would take a page out of my book and care for each other. I want to be remembered as a friend to everyone."

Banana George is frequently honored at ski tournaments, especially when his grandson, Rob Blair, and his great-granddaughter, Hayleigh Blair, compete. They are carrying on the Blair family skiing legacy. Rob broke the Georgia State Men's Five trick record in July 2017. Hayleigh has been skiing in the Nationals since she was eight years old. She says that she learned to "go after life, to make life happen" from her great-grandfather. It has helped her be a fierce competitor.

George's four daughters, four grandchildren, and four great-grandchildren continued to visit him at home. JoAnne had amazing caregivers for him around the clock. They did not just do the necessities but tended to him as they would their own father. Although they hadn't known him when he was a non-stop barefooting celebrity, they all loved him dearly. They seemed to intuit his former dynamic, loving character.

George passed peacefully at home in his sleep on October 17, 2013.

Memorial Service

The Memorial service for Banana George Blair was held in Red Bank, New Jersey at the John E. Day Funeral Home. He had made this request many years before because the family of his barefooting buddy, Chuck Sidun, owned the business at that time.

There was an overwhelming response to George's passing from friends and fans from around the world who had been touched by George's multi-faceted interests—his business and banking, and his community and sports activities—for over sixty years in the Red Bank area. At the Memorial Service, many people shared their heartfelt stories about George as their boss, as their teacher/mentor, as an ice boater, as a snow and water skier, as a drummer, and as an innovative thinker.

George's Eulogy by Carrie Blair

My father had a painful, crippling back condition, which constricted his life considerably. When spinal fusion corrected that in 1953, he discovered water skiing. He was exhilarated by this new sport that he could pursue on the Navesink River near his office in Red Bank, New Jersey.

He so fully became an athlete that everyone forgot he had recently been a cripple.

His family quickly embraced his excitement and formed Family Ski School in Red Bank and Mirror Lake in Edison, New Jersey, which was active for nineteen years.

Our family of six skied behind a boat as the opening act in ski shows with the Jersey Ski-Ters Club—stair-step in height, George, Dorothy, Donna, GeeGee, Carrie, Robin—in matching bathing suits.

We learned newly-invented tricks, tried the newest equipment, and usually had the fastest boat. George quickly became a local, then national, then international show-off, widening his circle of friends and fans.

His repertoire included kite flying over water on flat wing and then Delta kites, slalom, tricks, shoe skis, endurance, doubles with ladies on his shoulders, air chair, hydrofoil, barefoot jumping and slalom, tumble turns, backward face-down starts in the water, jumping from a fifteen-foot platform into the water, and his signature Rope-in-Teeth trick.

For a little guy, he had huge ambition, and an unlimited appetite for fun, constantly challenging himself to try the untried.

He spent his forties, fifties, sixties, seventies, eighties, and one-third of his nineties touring the world, becoming an ambassador of barefoot water skiing on size nine feet.

That's fifty-five years of public appearances, television interviews, teaching in many countries, being a guest of royalty, and speaking the universal language of sports competition worldwide. He knew everyone in the water ski world and everyone loved him.

George carried the torch of extreme sports well into what most would consider old age. He collected new sports like surfboarding, and snowboarding in Steamboat Springs, Colorado, with his grandsons, Rob, Marcus, Ted, and Oliver.

Cypress Gardens was his home for years, the Aqua Maids and Strong Men his buddies. He valued his locker there as one of his most cherished possessions because it allowed him to play among "up-and-coming" ski champions.

He was photographed with, and by, millions of people from all parts of the world in his loud yellow ski suits and clothes. He wore yellow shirts, pants, shorts, hats, boots, sunglasses, and tuxedos.

A natural leader in everything he engaged in, precise and demanding, he instilled loyalty in his employees and students. He looked for the best qualities in himself and others, built them up, and shared them—and wanted you to do the same.

His super-charged energy gave him a unique position as the poster boy of American water skiing, barefooting, and senior athletes. Ski tournaments and shows always had a ready draw when Banana George was the guest or featured skier.

His aging actually improved him, his beloved spotlight allowed him to spread his message of healthy eating and exercise and having a passion for life.

His energy created a vortex that drew crowds to him. He lived courage and optimism.

He recovered over and over from athletic injuries, impressing his doctors with his power of recuperation far beyond expectations.

JoAnne's sincere dedication contributed to his longevity. Her perennial optimism and ability to laugh away any setbacks supported his success.

He kept setting the bar higher and higher and didn't stop learning.

Fans old and young, fat and thin, able and not—all got a boost from watching him; they basked in his orbit. He was thrilling and terrifying to watch; controlled insanity seemed to describe him. I called him the "Oldest Jock in the World."

Most people have "fire in the belly" for a short, youthful spurt and soon give it up, satisfied, complacent, lazy. George knew how to raise his endorphin levels, enjoying a natural high. George never lost his fire. He taught us to love life, be bold, take risks, thrive on thrills, test ourselves, accept challenges, be unique.

George made friends all over the world and happily introduced himself to new people all the time, spreading good cheer.

His mission gave his life purpose and pleasure. His ninety-eight years flew by, starting practically when cars were invented and ending when smartphones were in everyone's hands. He was always excited about tomorrow and seeking the next adventure.

If you judge a person's life by the show of support, by the quality of those who come to celebrate that life, then you all are part of a legacy George carefully nurtured and wants you all to continue. We have a legend to live up to.

This email message, from a fan in Turkey, was read after the eulogy. On October 20, 2013, George's family received the following email:

> I met George on 2nd of May 1999 at Ataturk Airport Istanbul, Turkey. Fortunately, I was standing next to him and as he looked so happy I smiled as he gave me his business card with his story on it. He told me that everything is possible if you want it. He has given me such an inspiration that I've always talked about him when somebody told me that "they can't do...." As I told him that "I want to be like him." Three days ago, I told my husband that I'm scared of getting old and then remembered that lovely, full of life charismatic man and took the postcard he gave me and put it next to my computer. Now I found out that he passed away on the day I remembered him. (I'm sad and happy in a way.)
>
> I'm writing to you to express my sympathy and I'm sorry for your loss. I think he lived happy and gave happiness and hope to others—at least to me. I'm a Professor at a University and tomorrow I will tell my students about him and remember and pray for his soul.

God Bless You All
Best Regards,
Dr. Dilistan Çilingiroğlu Shipman

George's burial took place at Fairview Cemetery in Middletown, New Jersey, immediately after the memorial gathering. The pallbearers were: Rob Blair, Hayleigh Blair, Marcus Turrisi, Ted and Oliver Fetter, Alan Lopez, Bernie Yaged, and Chuck Sidun. A dinner reception followed at George's former New Jersey home on Buttonwood Drive, Shrewsbury.

In 2014, Banana George Blair was awarded, posthumously, the Hall of Fame Special Lifetime Tribute to celebrate his life as an "ambassador" for having made "an extraordinary impact on the sport." The family established a George Blair Ambassador Scholarship fund with the USA Water Ski Education Foundation to be awarded annually.*

In a condolence letter, Jim Grew, USA-Water Sports President, wrote, "The scholarship is a forever legacy that George so richly deserves." Grandson Robert Blair, following in his grandfather's footsteps, serves on the scholarship fund's Board of Trustees. To donate to the scholarship fund, go to the www.usa-wwf.org, click on Scholarship, and choose George Blair.

The family designed a bench cemetery marker in jet black granite. The god Mercury is etched in gold in the center. Bare footprints are carved on the front edge with the words *Barefootin' Banana George*. It is also inscribed with the song title "I Found My World in You" and a measure of the musical notes for the song, which exemplifies JoAnne's devotion to George.

*Recipients
2014 Paul O'Hara
2105 Jessica Trygier
2016 Erika Lang
2017 Erika Lang

Banana George's Lessons on Life

1. **Your Body:** Take care of your body. It is your most valuable asset, more valuable than your car, your house, your stocks and bonds.
2. **Hygiene:** Maintain scrupulous personal hygiene. Keep your body, hair, teeth, hands, and feet clean. Use a bidet.
3. **Nutrition:** Be mindful about what goes into your mouth. Make healthy choices of natural, fresh food and drink lots of water.
4. **Work:** Find work that engrosses you. It will follow that the harder you work, the happier you'll be.
5. **Imagination:** The future depends on ideas; imagination improves the world.
6. **Stress:** If you enjoy what you're doing, then you don't feel stress.
7. **Money:** As a banker, I make money by loaning money. But I believe that people should live within their means. As soon as you start borrowing money, you're borrowing trouble.
8. **Focus:** Be focused on your passion. You have to have a plan every day.
9. **Goals**: Set long-term, short-term, and daily goals.
10. **Curiosity/Learning:** Be curious, but not quite so curious as Curious George. Never stop learning. Try new things each day.
11. **Business:** Be honest with every decision; consider its risks and benefits. Always provide quality so you'll be proud of what you do.
12. **Service:** Do it right the first time so you will not have service issues. The customer is always right.
13. **Attitude:** Be positive, smile, laugh, spread happiness.
14. **Family:** Spend quality time with your family and take care of them first.
15. **Teach:** Share what you know with others so they can benefit from your experience.
16. **Retirement:** It is not a word in my vocabulary. What do you want to retire from? Life?

Countries Where Banana George Skied and/or Barefoot Water Skied

Antarctica
Aruba
Australia
Austria
Barbados
Bermuda
Bora Bora
Brazil
Bulgaria
Canada
Columbia
Costa Rica
Cuba
Curacao
Denmark
Egypt
England
Finland
France
French Guiana
Gambia
Germany
Gibraltar
Grand Bahamas
Grand Cayman
Greece
Haiti

Honduras
India
Italy
Jamaica
Jordan
Kenya
Lebanon
Martinique
Mexico
Monaco
Morocco
Nassau
New Zealand
Norway
Puerto Rico
Russia
Senegal
South Africa
Spain
Sweden
Switzerland
Tobago
Trinidad
Turkey
United States
Venezuela
Virgin Islands

Businesses Owned by Banana George

Founder/Owner	1946	DEBware
Founder/Owner	1948	Fogging Unlimited
Founder/Owner	1949	Hospital Portrait Service
Founder/Owner	1957	Scotch Scooters
Founder/Owner	1958	Family Ski School
Founder/Owner	1960	Boat, Ski & Scooter Center
Distributor	1960	American La France
Distributor	1962	Pyrotronics
Founder/Owner	1969	The Microfilm Center
Partner	1970	West Acres MH Park
Founder/Chairman	1970	Blair Trading Company
Founder/Vice Chairman	1974	Shrewsbury State Bank

Banana George's Affiliations and Memberships

Community

    Fellow, Metropolitan Museum of Art

    Director, Community Advisory Board, Monmouth Council of Girl Scouts

    President, Shrewsbury Borough Parent-Teacher Association

    Director, Monmouth County Tuberculosis Control Board

    Director, Red Bank Area Chamber of Commerce

    Director, Red Bank Community Appeal

    Foreman, Monmouth County Grand Jury

    Honorary Director, Distinguished Service Award, President, American Lung Association of Central New Jersey

    Member of Screen Actors Guild and American Federation of Television and Radio Artists

    Honorary Life Member, Professional Photographers of America

    Honorary Life Member, Society of Photographic Scientists and Engineers

    President, Association of Newborn Baby Photographers

    Member Emeritus, American Mosquito Control Association

    Member Emeritus, Biological Photographic Association

    Member, Social Register, New York City

    Member, Lake Region Yacht and Country Club

    Member, Delta Upsilon Fraternity

    Member, US Ski and Snowboard Association

    Charter Member, Pilots International Association

    Commodore, North Shrewsbury Ice Boat and Yacht Club

    Member, Skate Sailing Association of America

    2000: Snowboard Ambassador, Steamboat Springs

Water Ski

Trustee, American Water Ski Educational Foundation

Member, World Water Ski Union

Guest Star, Cypress Gardens Water Ski Show

Ambassador, Life Member, American Water Ski Association

Man of the Year, American Barefoot Club, 1982, 1986, 1987, 1992

American Water Ski Hall of Fame, inducted in 1991, the first barefooter admitted

Order of Merit, International Water Ski Federation, 2003

1988 *Guinness Book of World Records*, Barefoot water skied all seven continents, age 73

2003 *Guinness Book of World Records*, Oldest Barefoot Water Skier, age 88

2004 *Guinness Book of World Records*, Oldest Barefoot Water Skier, age 89

2005 *Guinness Book of World Records*, Oldest Barefoot Water Skier, age 90

2006 *Guinness Book of World Records*, Oldest Barefoot Water Skier, age 91

Contributors

EXCEPTIONAL GRATITUDE is due to Lynn Novakofski whose quick shutter captured George's essence over the years. During preparation of this book he was helpful in answering our technical questions.

Our deepest appreciation to the warmhearted caregivers who gave tender care to George in his final days.

Thanks also to George Severini of Dorn's Classic Photos for his expertise in preparing the photographs for publication.

The authors wish to extend a special thank you to all the contributors to this book who shared their memories.

Gordy Anderson
Swami Atmananda
Garry Barton
Kathy Bailey
Chris Beissinger
Stephen Beissinger
Leo Bentz
John Biffar
Zenon Bilas
Hayleigh Blair
Jessica Blair
Robert Blair
Shellie Blum
Heather Bonney
Lane Bowers
Don Buffa
Jennifer Calleri
John Clemmons
Danny Conner
Johnathan Conner
John Cornish

Cy Cyr
Ted Eisenstat
Sebastian Eggert
William Farrell
Frank Fetter
Oliver Fetter
Theodore Fetter
Robin Fitzmaurice
Richard Gray
Yvan Godard
Claudine Godard
Chip Hall
Rick Holland
Terry Ingram
Phil Keoghan
Billy Kidd
Bonnie Liss
Alan Lopez
Andy Lundt
Lori Lyons (Eckert)
Nick Mazza

Kathy McClintock
Mike Murphy
Judy Myers
Lynn Novakofski
Linda Sahagen Nunes
Char Portman
Paul Oman
Gene Quigley
Kuno Ritchard
Charles Sampson
Ron Scarpa
Chuck Sidun

Mike Siepel
David Small
Keith St. Onge
Al Turrisi
Marcus Turrisi
Mark Voisard
Jim White
Shirley White
Kathy Wolcott
Bernard Yaged
Alain Zrihen

Bibliography

The events, thoughts, quotes, and information for this book were compiled from interviews, personal notes, memorabilia, newspaper articles, videos, recordings, books, and magazines. Some of the sources are unknown and we have done our best to cite as many known sources as we can.

Books

Canfield, Jack and Mark Victor Hansen. *Chicken Soup for the Golden Soul: Heartwarming Stories about People 60 and Over.* Deerfield Beach, FL: Health Communications, 2000.

Darden, Bob and W. R. Spence, M. D. *December Champions.* Waco, TX: WRS Pubs, September 1993.

Ferrin, Kelly. *What's Age Got to Do With It?* San Diego, CA: ALTI Publishing, 1999.

Keoghan, Phil and Warren Berger. *No Opportunity Wasted: 8 Ways to Create a List for the Life You Want.* n.p.: Rodale Books, 2006.

Kita, Joe. *Wisdom of Our Fathers.* n.p.: Rodale Press, 1999.

McGrath, Don. *50 Athletes Over 50.* Denver, CO: Wise Media Group, 2010.

Stanton, Brandon. *Humans of New York.* New York, NY: St. Martin's Press Books, 2013.

Articles

"Banana George Skis to 92 With Style." *The Ledger.* January 22, 2007.

"Banana George Still Going Strong at 90." *The Monmouth.* September 24, 2004.

"Bananza Time." *News Chief.* October 2, 2005.

"Barefoot George Blair." *The Water Skier.* July/August 1986.

"Barefoot Mr. Banana." *Soviet Sports.* September 14, 1988.

"Barefoot Safari Across Africa." *The Water Skier.* July/August 1982.

"Blair Essentials." *The Ledger.* October 2, 2005.

"But Can He Walk on Water?" *USA Today.* February 2, 1990.

"George Blair Becomes Park Mayor." *News Chief*. January 22, 2006.

"George Blair Purchases the Boat Center." *Red Bank Register*. September 15, 1960.

"Impossible is Possible for Skier, 88." *Orlando Sentinel*. September 28, 2003.

"Ripening with Age." *The Ledger*. January 22, 2002.

"74-Year-Old Travels the World on Water Skis." *Tampa Tribune*. January 23, 1989.

"Ski-less Skiers to Compete Today." *The Ledger*. October 3, 2003.

"Star Attraction of Busch Gardens is on Skis." *The Senior Times*. August 22, 1990.

"Steamboat "Bananas" Over Blair." *The Steamboat Pilot*. June 28, 1990.

"The Adventures of Banana George." *Surfing Magazine*. September 1998.

"The Man Behind the Yellow Suit." *Essay*. 2003.

"The Ski's No Limit." *Lansing State Journal*. July 5, 1990.

"This Man Is Bananas About Waterskiing." *The Montreal Gazette*. August 16, 1990.

"Unusual Items in Articles Lead to Full Range of Unique Pursuits." *Long Branch Daily Record*. February 27, 1961.

"Water Skier Likes Ride on Wild Side." *St. Louis Dispatch*. July 16, 1990.

About the Authors

The Blair Family

George (center) with Robin, Carrie, GeeGee, Donna, and JoAnne.

Photo credit: Jim Reme

JoAnne Blair formerly worked in television programming and publishing. She was George's devoted wife for forty years. She lives in New York City.

Donna Blair is a retired Registered Nurse who now trains her German Shepherd in Schutzhund. She has a son (Rob and his wife Crystal) and two granddaughters (Jessica and Hayleigh).

Georgia Blair, a retired Registered Nurse and Midwife, is a hospice volunteer, EMT, and women's rights networker. She has a son (Marcus and his wife Jennifer) and two grandsons (Antonio and Nicholas).

Carrie Blair is a career equestrian, Tai Chi instructor, and field botanist who teaches plant identification.

Robin Blair, a former professional ballet dancer, is a conservationist and social justice activist. She has two sons (Theodore and Oliver and his wife Erin).

Karen Putz is a mom, writer, transformational speaker, Passion Mentor and barefoot water skier. She specializes in helping others unwrap their passions. Karen grew up hard of hearing and became deaf from a fall while barefoot water skiing. She is the author of *Gliding Soles* and *Unwrapping Your Passion* and a contributor to *Chicken Soup for the Soul*.

For further information about Banana George
and to stay connected, visit:

Facebook: https://www.facebook.com/BananaGeorgeBlair/

Website: www.BananaGeorgeBlair.com

Email: barefoot@bananageorgeblair.com